Sarah's Seasons

A Bur Oak Original

❖ ❖ ❖ ❖ ❖ ❖ ❖

Sarah's Seasons

An Amish Diary

& Conversation

❖ ❖ ❖ ❖ ❖ ❖ ❖

By Martha Moore Davis

University of Iowa Press   ᴪ   Iowa City

University of Iowa Press, Iowa City 52242

Printed in the United States of America

http://www.uiowa.edu/~uipress

Printed on acid-free paper

Library of Congress Cataloging-in-Publication Data
Davis, Martha Moore
    Sarah's seasons: an Amish diary and conversation / by
Martha Moore Davis.
        p.   cm.—(A Bur oak original)
    Includes bibliographical references.
    ISBN 0-87745-596-1
    1. Fisher, Sarah—Diaries.   2. Amish—Iowa—Kalona
Region—Diaries.   3. Amish women—Iowa—Kalona
Region—Diaries.   4. Kalona Region (Iowa)—Social life
and customs.   I. Fisher, Sarah.   II. Title.   III. Series.
F629.K25D39   1997
977.7'923—dc21   97-10556

02   01   00   99   98   97   C   5   4   3   2   1

FOR STEVE AND STEPHEN

Contents

Foreword

.

This is an appreciative foreword written from across the distances. They are the distances that still exist between rural village life and urban life, perhaps particularly life in a city like New York. They are the distances that exist between a secular existential thinker and a religious woman who writes within the fabric of a tradition, who lives in interlocking circles protected from the anguish of free choice. For all that, the voice of the living woman Sarah is made audible here. She is, even though she does not choose to advertise it, a creative person; and this frees her, although she may not know it, from the confines of doctrine and communally required compliance with predetermined rules.

She is Amish. The very word summons up, for many, the images of archaism, images of separation. And yet, because we associate the Amish culture with a peace and simplicity we realize we have lost, there is a pull at least to imagine how it is with them and how it was. How *does* the past work in their present? How and why do they survive?

Martha Davis enables us to feel ourselves into aspects of that world by linking her own lived experiences and even her own diary to what she presents of the Amish Sarah, writing the concrete particularities of her life. Because Sarah's voice and, yes, Martha's voice are contrasted to the voices of the social and educational historians who have "explained" what are called the Old Order Amish, we are struck by the peculiar mode of understanding made possible by diaries and letters. In this case, because the way of living, thinking, and communicating seems so remote from the contemporary, the reader cannot but be fascinated by the unfamiliar aspects, even as the same reader may be recognizing aspects of her or his familiar life.

At a moment of incoherence in our society and a prevailing sense of eroded communities, there is something stirring and, at once, suggestive in reading about an enduring community that looks (at least on the surface) like the paradigmatic New England community. The very ideas of the circles that are created by letter writing, the multiplicity of them, the striving toward consonance and understanding among participants—all these offer new perspectives on what communities may mean and how they might be created and sustained. The woman's vantage point cannot be undervalued here. The fact that Sarah, as a woman, is declaring herself as something other than the abstraction emerging from social science description connects her to the women's narratives that are appearing on all sides. She is refusing labeling here, Amish or not, rural or not. By the end, a reader finds herself crossing the distances. She cannot identify or (in some cases) even justify. But the world is wider for the experience and new human possibilities are disclosed.

Maxine Greene, Teachers College, Columbia University

Acknowledgments

I am grateful to Sarah Fisher and her family for sharing and for allowing me to explore their stories. I am also indebted to Anna Swartz, whose hospitality is an example for all.

Special thanks to Judy Goodwin for her responses to the stories. I am grateful to Julie Grask for her thoughts and to her daughter, Audrey, for reading diaries aloud. Thanks to Sheryl Shaver and Linda Phipps for their interest and knack for posing questions. I am grateful to Terri West for her insightful responses.

Finally, I thank Steve and Stephen for encouraging me and for building our own cache of stories.

Sarah's Seasons

1 Coming to Know Sarah

I only light the lamps if really necessary and not until dusk.
The windows in each room help a lot.

Sarah Fisher

I agonized over asking her. What if my question sounded too personal? Would I insult her? I knew the Old Order Amish valued their privacy away from mainstream life. At the same time, I felt an unspoken camaraderie with this Amish woman I had talked with only one other time.

I had met Sarah Fisher on a visit to Fellowship School about four months earlier. I was conducting postdoctoral research on Amish schools, and we had visited briefly. Now we were together again, enjoying an after-service Sunday dinner with nearly fifty other people at the home of David and Bertha Overholt.

"Have you ever kept a diary?" I blurted.

"Yes, several. Would you like to read them? Here, have some bread and pass it on," Sarah said.

The noon dinner continued, and so did our conversation. "Right now I'm not keeping a diary because I'm very busy with the baking business, but I'll show you the one I kept when I was first married. I just need some time to find it in my attic."

I learned later that Sarah, who I had thought to be about my age, was ten years older than I. She had written daily entries on a feed calendar for 1976 and 1977, each entry about five to six lines in length. At the time she began keeping the diary in January 1976, she had been married for two years, was thirty-four years old, had a daughter, Katie, two months old, and lived with her husband, Eli, on their farm. Sarah grew up on a farm in the Amish community near Kalona, Iowa. As is typical of Amish children, she attended Amish schools, and her formal education was completed through the eighth grade. She moved to Ohio to teach when she was twenty-one, taught for nine years, and then returned and married Eli at age thirty-two, relatively later than most Amish women, who usually marry in their twenties.

Although I was curious about Sarah's diary, what was foremost on my mind was why she trusted me to take it home with me to read. I was a mainstream outsider—an English person, as the

Amish say. Did she feel the unspoken bond between us that I did? And what about my own diary? Would she ever want to see it? I went home to my two old trunks filled with keepsakes to search for the five-year diary I had kept as a child and a travel diary I had kept as an adult. I hadn't looked at them in years. Why had I written them, and why did I still have them? And why had Sarah written and stored her diary? I found the idea of reading her diary gripping. Would I find relief from the overwhelming life I seemed to be leading?

Perhaps I felt compelled to reevaluate how I was going about daily living because of several events that occurred all at once. First I heard that an artist I admired had died of AIDS. Then an old friend told me he was HIV positive. Public service announcements about this disease were suddenly personal, not distanced educational campaigns. Finally I learned that the country church near Iowa City I had attended during my first eighteen years was closing. St. Bridget's Catholic Church, 105 years old, the anchor I thought would always be there, was no more.

But Sarah's rural community, older than St. Bridget's, was and is a vibrant one in which families combine efforts to pay hospital bills, to build new barns, and to serve food to hundreds of relatives at funerals. Sarah goes about living with assurance and peace, always knowing how to comfort others in the midst of hardships. Like Sarah, I had enjoyed a ready-made rural community during my farm upbringing in the fifties and sixties. My farm neighborhood included many friends and relatives living close to us, some less than a mile away. Sarah grew up learning to stitch a quilt at the quilting circles; I learned to sew at St. Bridget's Altar and Rosary Society meetings, where we made placemats for retirement homes. My relatives visited one another often. But how different the nineties are for me now, with my friends and relatives living all over the world. Naturally occurring conversations are fewer and fewer. Instead of talking with neighbors about the best grass seed to use, we hire lawn services that mechanically complete the tasks and move on to the next job.

It takes deliberate action to build shared experiences and communities. Sarah, her four girls, three boys, and husband Eli tell stories around the supper table about their work on the farm and in school. They talk over what they have learned from neighbors while attending a Sunday-night singing, and they listen to a visiting grandfather describe the first team of horses he worked. What stories will my son, Stephen, tell in twenty years? Are my husband Steve and I providing a community for him in today's world?

I cannot relate in a clever, twenty-second sound bite what Sarah has taught me about how to live within a community that places priority on people. When Sarah and I discuss such things, it usually takes two hours. That is how long it takes to pick the six rows of green beans in her garden. When we visit, talk and work go together. In this ongoing journey with Sarah, I become a member of a community in which I begin as an outside researcher and then find friendship. Through Sarah, I learn ways of living that dramatically change the way I live in the mainstream.

Our First Encounter

Sarah Fisher and I met in 1992 on an Amish school visitor's bench. I knew that the Amish welcome all visitors to their schools, but I hoped for more than just one or two visits. As a recent graduate of Teachers College, Columbia University in New York, I had accepted a college teaching position and begun work on postdoctoral research titled "The Old Order Amish in Iowa: Their Communities and Literacies." I planned to contrast the Old Order Amish schools near Kalona, Iowa, with mainstream schools to understand the ways communities support learning.

I knew I had to gain access in a courteous and proper way to build the necessary trust and a long-lasting relationship. A friend of mine introduced me to his aunt, Anna Swartz, a retired farm woman living in the Kalona area. Anna's family had been Old Order Amish until she was three, when her family became Mennonite and chose a less conservative lifestyle. Though she grew up with motorized vehicles, telephones, and electricity (all modern conveniences not used by the Old Order Amish), she maintains close relationships with her Amish relatives. Anna arranged visits to several Amish schools, and together, we launched my study.

One early fall morning I drove from my home in Des Moines to the Kalona area to pick up Anna. We then drove to the one-room Fellowship School. Entering the room quietly, we found a woman already on the visitor's bench. I assumed it was the mother of one or more of the pupils, or scholars, as the Amish children are called. She signed the visitor's book and handed it to me. She had written her name and a comment: "Sarah Fisher. It's a bright, sunny day." Several people had been there that month. I skimmed over the entries, and then followed suit. After signing my name, I wrote "We are enjoying our visit," and I passed the book on to Anna. At recess time we filed outside with the scholars. As the children played tag, the adults visited.

With recess over, Sarah said, "I have to walk home now. I have gardening to start and bread rising at home, and I need to bake it. During the summer months I bake for the Farmers' Market, but now, during fall and winter, we sell our goods at the weekly auction."

"What do you bake? Where is the auction? How much do you bake?" I asked. I found out that the Fishers have a year-round baking business. Did Sarah operate it? Could an Amish woman have her own business? There were so many more questions I wanted to ask. Suddenly the activities and routine of Fellowship School seemed unimportant. I offered to give Sarah a ride home, and she accepted. (Anna later explained that it is common for the Amish to accept an occasional ride and also to hire drivers for long-distance trips.) I kept asking questions, and she kept answering them. As I dropped Sarah at her farmhouse, she said, "Come back and visit and we can talk some more."

A major snowstorm hit. Severe, subzero temperatures set in. My family's schedule and my teaching kept me planning and coordinating activities at home. Several months went by. Finally, one dreary, cold Sunday in February 1993, I overcame my hectic schedule, and Anna and I arranged to attend an Amish church service together. That week's service was held at David and Bertha Overholts' house. Afterward we hoped to stop at Sarah's home to visit.

The Amish church service consisted of singing, praying, and a sermon, the men seated in the living room and the women in the dining room. The very young children were attended to by both fathers and mothers, who sometimes left to put a sleepy child in a nearby bedroom. True to Amish tradition, a light dinner was served at noon after the service. The Overholts had planned for two seatings, one in the basement and one in the dining room, to accommodate the fifty or more people in attendance. Anna and I were invited to eat at the dining room table, and to my delight, I was seated next to Sarah Fisher.

As we passed around pickled red beets, a stack of sliced, homemade wheat bread, peanut butter with marshmallow cream added, egg salad, and butterscotch pie, we became reacquainted. The unspoken bond I felt with this Amish woman gave me the courage to ask if she kept a diary. Much later, I told Sarah that I called this second meeting the Diary Conversation. I asked her why she had offered to let me read her diary. She said, "Well, you said you were a teacher. I knew from the way you talked you like to learn. So do I."

Yes, we had that in common. There were immense dissimilarities in the way we lived our lives: her Amish service and my Catholic Mass; her buggy and my car; her German language and my English. The list was endless. But none of that mattered. We spoke the same language, that of diary keeping.

The Diary in the Attic

Sarah and I sat in front of the heating stove in her living room. Straight from Sarah's attic storage, the booklet I held felt icy to the touch. It was a feed calendar. Anxiously I opened it and began to read.

I hoped my face didn't reveal my disappointment. The entries were so spare. What significance could this diary possibly have?

June 22, 1976. Last night a thief came & stole the bigger lame chick. Maybe it was a raccoon. I grabbed the flashlight but neither could I see nor hear of it anymore in the dark. I pulled weeds in the cane patch.

June 23, 1976. Eli sold pigs at the Sale Barn [a weekly livestock sale in the town of Kalona]. I washed windows indoors & out, and washed off other things in the kitchen. Katie can crawl over the floor fast.

July 21, 1976. The relief sewing was here. Was cloudy most of the day. We quilted under the tent in P.M. Attendance in all was over 50 (large).

Did I need to break some kind of code in order to glean any understanding? The diary entries were minimal and almost terse. It would be rude to say this to Sarah; I didn't know what to say. I smiled and thanked her for lending them to me.

"Take the diary with you so that you can really read it and think about it. Then, when you're done, come back to visit and you can return it," Sarah said.

I drove away from Sarah's farmhouse feeling a sense of responsibility to protect the diary and honored that she would trust me to take it home with me. Yet what was I protecting except a mundane record?

Later, while driving to campus for class one warm winter day, I found myself hoping for snow to cross-country ski. Suddenly

THESE FEATURES MAKE THE AUDIT WEEKLY THE MOST POPULAR REMINDER CALENDAR IN ITS FIELD

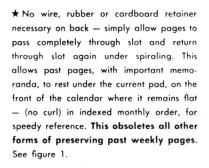

★ No wire, rubber or cardboard retainer necessary on back — simply allow pages to pass completely through slot and return through slot again under spiraling. This allows past pages, with important memoranda, to rest under the current pad, on the front of the calendar where it remains flat — (no curl) in indexed monthly order, for speedy reference. **This obsoletes all other forms of preserving past weekly pages.** See figure 1.

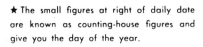

★ The small figures at right of daily date are known as counting-house figures and give you the day of the year.

★ The bar in spiral wire makes for easier turning of pages and anchors the pad securely under metal strips at side of slot.

I kept my diary on what was handy—a feed calendar.—Sarah Fisher

I thought of something Sarah had written: "January 23, 1976. Beautiful. No snow. Would be nice to have real winter again. . . . 65 in P.M." Why would Sarah want colder weather?

The following Saturday morning I sat in our breakfast room and read through several months of Sarah's faithful entries. Occasionally I watched the cardinals on our bird feeder in the frozen flower garden, and questions flooded my mind: Where did Sarah read in her house? Where and what time of day did she usually write in her diary? What did she feel? How could she find the time to write, day after day?

Over the next several months, I read Sarah's diary over and over. The more I read, the more I wondered about the missing details. I made lists of questions to ask Sarah. What does gma mean? Why are singings noted so often? Why are a man and woman's names written together, such as Bill Clara?

I began to visit Sarah on a regular basis. I would send a card two weeks in advance, naming a day on which I planned to stop for a visit. If that particular day wouldn't work, she would drop a card to me or make a phone call from a neighbor's to reschedule. We split our time together between household chores and talk of other topics. We baked pies, shelled peas, picked strawberries, whatever Sarah's work was that day. Though I knew something about the nature of garden and household tasks, my 1950s and 1960s upbringing had included modern conveniences like canned soups and electric mixers and blenders. Sarah's work was new to me.

At home, I read the diary silently and then aloud. Because I spent more time with Sarah, I began to hear her voice as I read the diary aloud. Her descriptions, however brief, said more than I had originally thought. It seemed significant, for example, when little or nothing was written, such as in an entry about the death of a loved one. Through reading parts of the diary more than once, I began to infer humor, exasperation, and sadness. And what was most surprising was that the urge to compare her life and diary to my own became even stronger.

Diary-Keeping Purposes

In my family, diary reading was *the* recreation. We'd push back our chairs from the supper table and my dad would say, "Let's have a look at some of those diaries." Out of the attic would come one of several gallon-size, metal ice-cream containers that stored my grandfather's diaries against the mice in our 1865 farmhouse.

Dad would pry off the lid with a pop. Like cream soda fizzing out of its glass bottle, out would spill the small, bound books, diaries written from 1915 to 1950. Dad would say, "Here's a year to think about: July 5, 1933. Humid; corn growing good. Ralph came over today to help with the hay. Finished the 40 acres. Got postcard from John—coming on the train Thursday from Chicago." Dad would read between the lines for us. Ralph was our cousin, an integral part of the family, and John was an uncle living in Chicago. We pondered life on an Iowa farm when my grandfather was a young man. Just beginning farming in the 1920s, he struggled to keep his eighty acres in spite of the Great Depression. During World War II he reflected on the absence of two of his three sons serving in the military. To me, these stories were just like those in the books on my fourth-grade classroom's autobiography shelf.

Then, as a nine-year-old, I was given a five-year diary for Christmas by my great-uncle Rob, who said, "You ought to keep this diary. It will be real interesting someday." I kept it faithfully from 1960 to 1965. It must have been important to me, because I found it years later in the bottom of a storage trunk. The diary's sage green cover was bordered in gold filigree and black trim, with a lion's head crest in the center. Underneath, the words "FIVE YEAR DIARY" were emblazoned in capital letters.

Reading excerpts of my diary along with Sarah's, I could see our priorities in what we recorded as the important events of a particular day. On April 15, 1977, Sarah wrote: "In A.M. I rocked both girlies showing Katie pictures from the *Bible Primer*. She liked the 'horsie' that carried Mary & Baby Jesus." On May 5, 1961, my diary says: "Shot a man into space. Came back alive. Name: Allen B. Shepard Jr."

One day I said, "Sarah, tell me some of the stories in your diary."

Sarah quickly responded, "But my diary isn't classified as a story. It references happenings. What person worked where. You tell when crops were ready in the garden."

"But why did you write your diary?" I asked.

"I didn't think about why I wrote it at the time. It was in our family, so I did it, too. It's sort of for records. It's mostly tradition. I can look back on things and see what went on. My children like to hear what they did when they were really young. I used my grandfather's to check back when I missed some days. He was very faithful in his writing. Sometimes I wanted to see what he thought about something. I checked for my birthday, and he hadn't written anything. Then the next day, he said, 'Henrys had a baby.' I was glad he had written about me.

"A diary can settle a question, a disagreement. If someone thought it was June 12—and no, it wasn't—it was June 15 when that happened, then your diary can show this. It settles arguments. You look back and see what took place. That's history. It gives reference. It helps when you want to know when something happened."

With permission I began to write down some of these conversations, setting aside current technology such as tape recorders, one of the many conveniences rejected by the Amish. Instead, I relied on pen, paper, and memory. What had been a field-study notebook for the purpose of preserving details about Amish schools became instead a diary of our visits. In Sarah's community I became an explorer each time I attended a local auction, a quilting, or a supper. I felt an intense accountability to Sarah and her husband, Eli. They were real people with feelings, not people to be "studied."

Often I had to ask myself, Was I conducting an inquiry about Amish schools and community, or was I seeking to understand Sarah in particular?

I consulted John Hostetler's *Amish Society* and found three references in the 402 pages specifically indexed under the word *women*. Four pages are devoted to women's dress. Five pages discuss the role of the woman in Amish society, describing her relationship to her husband and the church. One page tells of the Amish woman's role in agriculture. About the Amish woman Hostetler notes:

> For her satisfaction in life she turns to brightly colored flowers in the garden, or in the winter, to rug-making, embroidery work on quilts, pillowcases, and towels, and to shelves of colored dishes in her corner cupboard. Some, the work of her hands, are her prized possessions, made for the enjoyment of the household and her host of relatives.

I wondered specifically what Sarah would consider her satisfaction in life. Traditional sociological constructs could not furnish the information needed to understand this individual. Sarah's friendship led me naturally to learning through means I had previously not considered—diaries and conversations.

I put aside the scholarly frameworks. Meeting Sarah was the beginning of events and experiences I hadn't planned. What began as a carefully designed, formal postdoctoral study of mainstream and Amish schools changed into something much different. It became, instead, a story of the emerging friendship of two kindred spirits.

Special Notes about the Diary

Sarah Fisher's diary for 1976 and 1977 appears with her permission. She has not read my transcriptions, but we have had many discussions about her diary and her life, and about mine. Although not deliberately crafted as a literary work, her diary reveals an ongoing account of her daily routine, and a narrative emerges. I group Sarah's two-year diary entries chronologically a few months at a time. For example, January and February 1976 are followed by the corresponding months of 1977. I cluster the months in this way to highlight seasonal occurrences in her life as well as her many roles: Sarah the teacher, mother, and guide; Sarah the quilter; Sarah the gardener; Sarah the entrepreneur; Sarah the writer.

To highlight aspects of Sarah's life, I have included with permission some photographs and sketches. I took all the photos in natural light and respected Amish tradition and modesty, depicting objects and not people.

In order to maintain privacy and authenticity, I have used the technique Andrea Fishman devised for *Amish Literacy: What and How It Means*, in which pseudonyms are based on the common Amish names listed in Hostetler's *Amish Society*. I have also used Amish names that appear in documents of Sarah's community, such as family tree records and a local listing of Old Order Amish names and addresses. For each person named in Sarah's diary, I have assigned a pseudonym and maintained it consistently. About 290 people are mentioned in Sarah's diary at least once over a period of two years. For someone who travels by horse and buggy, Sarah regularly visits a remarkable number of family and friends. A typical entry from the diary is March 20, 1977, in which Sarah lists seven households as present. And then she adds: "I enjoyed having supper company." During the month of January 1976, she made twenty to twenty-five references to family and friends, sometimes to individuals, sometimes to entire households. The same is true for January 1977. I see many people each day, but I have never visited with twenty-five family and friends in a month, particularly the cold month of January.

In *Amish Society* Hostetler states that of the 144,000 Amish today, there are 126 family names. In the three largest communities—found in Pennsylvania, Indiana, and Ohio—more than half the population is accounted for with five names. In 1993 the Kalona post office needed to distinguish 450 Miller and 85 Swartzendruber families for mail delivery. The limited number of first and last names in Sarah's community can be seen in the "Johnson and Washington Counties Amish Addresses" booklet, published in 1992. It lists twenty-one head-of-household names, accounting for 179 households. Sarah said that as of 1996, there were 750 to 800 people in her Old Order Amish community. Usually twelve to fourteen people live within each household.

Sarah's community has many ways to identify people accurately. She pointed out, "With so many people of the same name, both first and last, it's crucial to know exactly who you are talking about." Families are referred to by the last name made plural— Fishers—or by the father's first name made plural; for example, "Elis came to visit" means that Eli's whole family visited. Sarah often refers to her own parents and siblings as "Dads" or "Pops." Sometimes she also adds a middle initial following a first name to ensure accurate identification; for example, "Norman Ts" refers specifically to Norman T and his family, as distinguished from another Norman and his family.

As another way to clarify, a family or the mother of that family is sometimes referred to with two names, the first the father's name and the second the mother's name. "Jonah Claras" refers to the family in which the father's name is Jonah and the mother's name is Clara. The singular form, "Jonah Clara," refers to the woman named Clara who is married to Jonah. Sarah sometimes refers to an entire family by using the three initials of the family's father written in capital letters; for example, "ESFs came to church" refers to the entire family of Eli Simon Fisher.

When Sarah explained all this to me, she said, "Now you try it. You're Martha, but here you'd be known as Steve Martha, because that's your husband's name. What would Anna be?"

"Clarence Anna, right?" I responded.

"Yes, now you understand." It would take some getting used to.

In editing the diary entries, I have made every attempt to maintain Sarah's original meaning based on the context in which she wrote. Though Sarah did not record the days of the week, I have added them so that the reader can more easily visualize Sarah's routines. Explanatory notes about her customs and culture are placed in brackets to provide perspective on the significance of some of the events. For example, on January 15, 1977, Sarah noted: "We had an auction among us to dispose of Joes' items outlawed in Missouri [items not allowed in the community where Joe's family was moving]."

Sarah made few or no erasures and lined through only a few words to indicate corrections. In watching Sarah fill out shopping lists or draw up sketches of her garden, I know that she writes quickly and accurately the first time, making few changes. Any parentheses in the diaries are Sarah's own; she used them occasionally to add extra explanations. I left abbreviations like & (and) as well as b-4 (before) intact. Sarah's playful use of abbreviations adds to the reader's sense of her personality. Similarly, I indicate in brackets where Sarah drew pictures to record the weather conditions or sights such as geese flying overhead.

Sarah sometimes wrote from the point of view of her young daughter. She drew the outline of Katie's hand and within the shape of it wrote as follows: "May 5, 1977. Mama should be washing dishes but she's writing in her diary. Baby [Katie's sister, Barbara] is sleeping in her white 6 year old crib. The mattress is up higher than mine. I get to sleep in the newer bed. My quilt has brown and tan. It matches with my bed. The mattress has puppies on it. Bye—Katie."

Sarah wrote some words in her dialect. I have placed the English words in brackets so that the reader can see exactly how she wrote the entries. The Old Order Amish commonly speak three languages—English, Pennsylvania German, and High German. In Sarah's community, teenagers learn High German in school. After the eighth grade they attend Dutch College, or additional sessions in High German, in preparation for their church services. With the non-Amish public, they speak English. Within their own community, they speak their dialect, Pennsylvania German, sometimes called Pennsylvania Dutch. This term is explained by J. William Frey in *A Simple Grammar of Pennsylvania Dutch*. He notes that the Amish came from German provinces but sailed from Holland on Dutch ships. When arriving in Philadelphia, they may have said the word *Deitsch* (their dialect form of the High German *Deutsch*), and the port authorities likely wrote the nearest English equivalent. In Sarah's community, this dialect is almost exclusively oral, but Sarah occasionally put selected words on paper. As she told me, "Once in a while, the right word is hard to come by, so sometimes I use a German word when I'm writing."

Sarah's writing style includes vivid, succinct descriptions of her daily routine and a knack for understatement that imparts disapproval: "Eli sat and talked with that Jehovah Witness woman plenty long." She expresses tiredness, and perhaps a desire for privacy: "We went away to avoid company, but arrived home and company came anyway!" Though subtle, Sarah's deliberate use of punctuation provides the reader with a window on her emotional responses: "And already the last day of Jan.!" She also reveals pride in her own accomplishments by reporting how many clothing items she has washed and how many cans of beans she has processed.

Occasionally Sarah notes that drivers transport her family to a funeral or to an auction in Iowa City, or that she makes a phone call from a neighbor's house. Although the Amish do not allow motorized vehicles, they do consider it permissible to hire a driver and vehicle to travel great distances, and to use a telephone for practical purposes, such as making a doctor's appointment. Sarah and her family travel via horse and buggy or wagon to do their shopping or trading in the town of Kalona and at several local grocery and general stores established for the convenience of the Amish community.

Sarah and I agree that it is surprising we didn't meet years ago, since we grew up in the same rural area. Our families' farms were only about twenty-five miles apart. Her ancestors and mine were immigrants who arrived in Iowa in the 1840s, hers from Germany for religious reasons and mine from Ireland for economic ones. Johnson and Washington counties make up the largest Old Order Amish settlement in Iowa. Sarah often visits the other Iowa communities located in Buchanan County, the Riceville-McIntire area, Bloomfield, the Milton-Pulaski area, and Lucas County, near the town of Chariton.

My experience was common to that of many mainstream people living close to an Amish community: we interacted very little. Living on our 160-acre farm from 1951 to 1969, I met only one Amish person. My job was to raise mallard ducks, and I sold them to an Amish farmer who lived about thirty miles from us. I remember the first time I met him in 1961. Early one summer morning, he arrived with his hired driver, who backed his old International truck up to the duck pens located alongside our maintenance shop, a former one-room schoolhouse. We loaded the ducks into slatted wooden crates.

Once the crates were stacked on the box of the truck, the Amish man pulled rolled-up bills out of his pocket and handed them to me. "Fifty dollars. A dollar a duck. Thank you." I remember holding the money, looking up at the tall Amish farmer, and responding with a proper "Thank you." He didn't look like any farmers I knew. He wore dark trousers, a light blue shirt, suspenders, and a straw hat not at all like the seed-corn caps other farmers wore. He had no mustache, but a long, black beard sprinkled with gray. I watched as he lifted the tailgate and slammed it shut, looped the two chains on either side of the tailgate up, and dropped the attached hooks into place. He turned and stepped into the truck. As the driver pulled away, the dust from the gravel lane blurred the sight of the wooden crates stacked on the bed of the pickup. A few feathers floated out of the crates and onto the dusty road. The ducks' quacking faded, and I was left with questions about the Amish farmer. Why did he dress that way? Didn't he know how to drive a truck himself? Why didn't the driver dress the way the Amish farmer did?

Years later, when I went to Fellowship School and sat on the visitor's bench, I was thinking back to that experience when Sarah leaned over and asked me, "Why are you interested in the Amish schools? You're already a teacher and your schools are different from ours. What can you learn from us?" I told her I had a feeling that I could learn a lot, though I wasn't sure what just yet.

Now, the question of why I want to be there has disappeared. Now Sarah says, "Here, let's roll out this pie crust," and we talk.

2 Sarah the Teacher: Mother and Guide

You ought to keep a diary.
Someday it will be real interesting.
Martha's great-uncle Rob

I felt like one of the Amish teachers attending their Friday-night meeting in Sarah's community. The teacher-host for the evening invited me to sit at one of the scholars' desks and try a worksheet on arithmetic.

I noticed that nearly everyone was finished, but I was still deliberating over several crossword clues. How many pecks were in a bushel? Go on to the next one. Now for addition and subtraction. I was slow, having become accustomed to using a calculator for computations. Calculators aren't allowed in the Amish schools, but it didn't appear that anyone needed them as the teachers rapidly wrote answers. I was relieved when a teacher in the desk next to me asked, "Would you like some help?"

The teachers introduced the topic: variations to break monotony in arithmetic drills. Later we sang German hymns, and the evening ended at about ten o'clock. I felt so accepted, having been included in everything from the teachers' work to stacking up my supper plate. The evening was made possible by Sarah and other parents, who brought the food and served the teachers. Sarah enjoyed such evenings herself as a teacher in Ohio.

I held Sarah's bonnet for her as she put on her shawl and picked up her dishes. Back at her farmhouse, Sarah's cousin Anna Swartz, Sarah, Eli, and I visited in the lantern light. Anna teased Eli: "See what you took Sarah away from. She could still be teaching if you hadn't married her!"

With no hesitation, and with a smile, Eli responded, "But I needed her!" We laughed but could hear the sincerity in his voice.

Though Sarah has left the schoolhouse, she has not left teaching. "What is the difference between this black dirt and this kind?" Sarah asked as she scooped up black dirt in one hand and orange dirt in the other.

"Different color and texture," I responded.

"Yes, I brought this orange dirt back from our trip to Oklahoma when we visited relatives. I'll plant watermelons here. They need easily drained soil to thrive, and this soil will help."

Much learning takes place outside school. Sarah gives her young children cardboard boxes that they transform into houses and barns. Sarah and her friends demonstrate tasks and tell stories: "What to do when sixty-five egg whites are left over after making noodles with the yolks for the farmer's market? Make angelfood cakes to sell, as well. I'll tell you about the first time my mother taught me to bake an angelfood."

"Those Look-Easy Jobs"

Sarah's work reminds me of what my great-uncle Rob used to call "those look-easy jobs." The same great-uncle gave me a diary and built farm fence out of woven wire and wooden posts in Cedar County. In 1962, when I was eleven and my brother was eight, we watched a new fence go in on our farm. Uncle Rob would pick up his posthole digger and start in as if he heard a drum cadence in his head. Thrusting the posthole digger into the earth, he would extract a load of dirt, swing around, release the two wooden handles, and drop the dirt in a pile. It looked like such fun.

After noon dinner, Ed and I would often follow the crew back to the field to watch. One day, during a water break under the hickory tree, I asked Uncle Rob if I could give it a try. The crew laughed at my naive request, but not Uncle Rob. He smiled and offered me first crack at the next hole. I confidently walked over to the posthole digger and found I couldn't even pick it up. Ed added his strength but still we couldn't.

"Seems to me it's one of those look-easy jobs. Here, let me give you a hand. I've been making fence for fifty-two years. It gets easier as you go along." Uncle Rob stepped in, and with our hands next to his, he thrust the posthole digger into the earth, and together we made a clean start on the next hole. Of course, I learned that there is much more to a task than might at first appear.

Sarah's daily life is consumed with look-easy jobs. She accomplishes her work with enthusiasm and commitment. Sarah learned her skills by watching demonstrations, sometimes from unlikely people. Sitting next to the heating stove in the living room as we warmed ourselves, she told me of learning how to crochet from a school friend's brother when she was a young girl. She went home with her friend for dinner, and the two girls were talking about starting a new project. In Sarah's words, the girl's brother started "showing off" to her. He claimed he knew how to crochet. "It's like tying up a horse," he said, and then described the process: "Pass the lines through the harness, then pull it up through, then with a pull, it all comes apart!" We laughed, and Sarah said, "He was actually correct—connecting his horse's harness really was a chain stitch like crocheting."

As we visited, Sarah's daughter Mary copied a sentence on a huge piece of slate attached to the wall facing the kitchen. "If you can't be thankful for the things you have, be thankful for what you don't have." Mary finished copying the sentence and then signed her name.

Sarah asked, "Have you ever heard this?" She read the saying from the chalkboard. We laughed. "I always like to write something on the chalkboard, something besides reminders to myself or to other members of the family. The children can practice writing their words and letters here, too."

As we watched Mary at work, Sarah offered me a piece of the brown bread she had made from a recipe I had given her. I use a Christmas pudding mold and steam it on top of the stove according to the directions, but Sarah adapted the recipe and baked hers in her oven in an angelfood cake pan. Even if I had time to think about it, I wouldn't have thought of an alternative cooking method and pan. I wouldn't have made the recipe at all.

"Do you see yourself as creative?" I asked Sarah.

"I do, but should you say it yourself?" she answered.

"Would others notice that you're creative?" I asked.

"If they look for it. Otherwise, no," Sarah said. "We're reminded of the need for humility in many ways." She pointed to an issue of *Family Life*, a magazine written by the Amish community. "This article, 'Me, Myself, and I,' urges us to work to overcome human nature. Egotism needs to be laid aside and humility and submission should find their rightful place."

Though Sarah is diligent in her modesty, her imagination comes through in her diary as well as in her actions. She writes with variety, sometimes referring to herself in the third person: "Mrs. Fisher washed, folded diapers, and other things." Rather than simply report that the children were with her, she writes, "My little maids sat side by side in basement opposite of me & helped with potatoes." Perhaps Sarah is creative because she is so practical. As Sarah says, "We learn best by doing. Our experience teaches us. I wouldn't know how to do it any other way."

After the teachers are done talking about teaching at their evening meeting, the parents bring in a hot meal. A haystack supper is more fun than a plain meal. Many times the teachers have a singing after they eat.—Sarah Fisher

AN AMISH SCHOOLTEACHER
SUPPER RECIPE: THE HAYSTACK

Place the following separate dishes out on a long table in the schoolroom:

slightly crushed potato chips or crackers
cooked baked beans
cooked crumbled hamburger
cooked sliced carrots
cooked cubed potatoes

Teachers file by the long table and stack up their dinner, one ingredient on top of the other, like a haystack of loose hay. Why? "Because it's more fun this way." Note: Place the dishes on the table, to be stacked on the dinner plate in an order that will allow for a base. For example, start with the potato chips or crackers.

MARTHA'S STEAMED BROWN BREAD

Mix together:

1 cup rye flour
1 cup corn meal
1 cup whole wheat flour
2 tsp. soda
1 tsp. salt
Stir in:
3/4 cup molasses
2 cups sour milk or buttermilk

Beat well. Fill greased molds 2/3 full (using two 1-lb. coffee cans or one 7″ tube mold). Lay waxed paper over the top. Steam 3 hours. Serve piping hot with butter.

"I make it in my Christmas pudding mold."—Martha
"I use my angelfood cake pan."—Sarah

January and February 1976

Thursday, January 1, 1976. Cloudy & windy. Rained in P.M. which made icy sidewalks. We had our Christmas dinner on the Miller side at Sams. Katie enjoyed being held and went way over nursing time.

Friday, January 2, 1976. Eli skated on way to work part ways. I finished a nighty for baby from material Ed Sarah gave. It has 2 sides, smooth & flannel. In eve. Billy Stuzman took a load of Fishers to Elroy Rabes.

Saturday, January 3, 1976. My, my how time flies. Baby was fussy until in eve. she slept & slept again. She has a chest cold, poor child. I washed dirty smear cheese [a spread made of milk curds and cream to be eaten on bread] dishes of yesterday. Eli washed the diapers for me & fixed the washing machine [Sarah's community allows gas-powered washing machines].

Sunday, January 4, 1976. Cold. Church at Fred Roy Yoders. Baby did well. Went to Jacobs in P.M. & were there for supper. Had pizza. Got home late.

Monday, January 5, 1976. Yeah bo! I was done washing by 11:15. Katie cooperated well. I hauled water for Marigold in the laundry cart & she really drank. The hens too were very thirsty & out of water. Pan was frozen. I watched them as they gathered around & bobbed their heads up & down. Got 14 eggs in A.M. Eli made crude nests but they're practical.

Tuesday, January 6, 1976. Done with chores by 10:45 A.M. (Surely is good for me to get fresh air.) Got 8 eggs, watered the animals & poured oats in bin to use for turkey house. Husband got up late so I finished chores after he'd gone & I washed dishes & washed baby. Chilly & cloudy.

Wednesday, January 7, 1976. Humpf. I'm down with the flu. It came on me last night. Felt dizzy, had abdominal pain & vomited.

Husband was alarmed. He kindly massaged me. The cold wind doth blow today & house seems none too warm at present. Eli went to Sale Barn. I took care of baby & me.

Thursday, January 8, 1976. 11 below. Nice to have a dry place to be. Snow on ground. Seems like winter. Poor babe has a hacking cough. I feel better, but am still weak. Eli went up to the home-place to butcher.

Friday, January 9, 1976. 0/5 [five degrees below zero] in morn, 38/0 [thirty-eight degrees above zero] in P.M. Brutish Marigold found her way out of her stall into the "fudder gang" [food, the hay] & stood there & looked at me when I came out to let her out of the barn. She squeezed herself back again & went outdoors not at all hungry as she stood & did nothing. Made Katie a royal blue dress from my apron and cape.

Saturday, January 10, 1976. Eli wanted to bake the eggs this morn because he wanted to do it his way. He did a nice job. Missie [Sarah's baby daughter, Katie] is gaining in intelligence—Coos more & wants to sit up straight. She says, "A-gu." Cloudy. Had meatloaf for dinner. I cleaned. Felt tired in P.M. Rested on sofa—baby with me. [On the bottom of the feed calendar page a sentence was printed: "They know enough who know how to learn." Sarah wrote next to it, "good thought."]

Sunday, January 11, 1976. Went to Jonah Clara & girls 4 a good dinner. Elmer Ks, Larry Bs, & Jerry Ys attended too. Ate popcorn in evening & drank cider. Eli read from *Martyrs Mirror* [a book containing stories of the martyrs; common reading among the Amish]. I wrote letter & played with baby.

Monday, January 12, 1976. Nice day—Almost like spring. 40 in A.M. Katie is lying on the sofa crying and was just playing with her patties a minute ago. Bologna is being canned in pressure cooker. 6 qt. are waiting. I sorted wash & should hop to it. 1 bologna jar broke in cooker! Am tired (evening).

Tuesday, January 13, 1976. I took Katie to Dr. Swenson in Cedar Rapids for her 2nd treatment. [About chiropractor treatments Sarah said, "We are a physical people doing work, have lots of aches, so go to chiropractors."] She cried again. Snowed here in A.M. but no snow in Cedar Rapids. I hung up wash in P.M. Lloyds & Jacobs got out 2 pigs & took up to homeplace for to kill.

Wednesday, January 14, 1976. We went up to homeplace to butcher. We had 2 pigs, Lloyds & Jacobs each 1. Joe, Mom, Abes, & ESFs [Eli Simon Fisher family] helped. We forgot to take lard containers & hamburger for the sausage along.

Thursday, January 15, 1976. Baby must be right-handed. I put her in the jumper for the 1st time & she reached for the wooden beads with right hand. Snowing. Am canning pork. I just can't trust my Mirrormatic Cooker. It's broken more jars already despite what I try! Lost 2 jars today. I put cider & molasses to mincemeat.

Friday, January 16, 1976. I bathed Missie. She loves to sit in the water & kick. She weighs 14 lbs. 12 oz. I lengthened Katie's pink dress already & fixed her slip so she can wear it. Also remodeled her Sunday cap from Peter Katie.

Saturday, January 17, 1976. Up & at it b-4 breakfast. Baked 2 mince pies, bread, & grapenuts today. Also cooked apples & chocolate pudding & canned 7 qt. meat, some with broth. Washed & washed dishes, filled lamps & brought in wood. Bathed & shampooed & ironed baby's apron & dress. To bed late.

Sunday, January 18, 1976. Church at Fred Roys. Scripture Matthew 4−5. Sermon by David. Went to William Fishers in P.M. Katie & I both wore lavender. Cold wind.

Monday, January 19, 1976. We sisters & sisters-in-law, Amos Lydie & Ivan Leah went to Bertha's quilting at Pops. Bill Bauff, Hattie took us except Ann, Barbara, & Lydie. I went uptown & bought dry goods, etc. Got a lunch pail for Eli's birthday.

Tuesday, January 20, 1976. 'Twas late until I got to laundering a big wash. Hung "straight wash" outdoors & tailored clothes in basement. Was plenty late to hang 'em out. Gathered up potatoes from cellar floor finally.

Wednesday, January 21, 1976. Eli & I went to ESFs. He went from there with Mark to Sale Barn. I sewed a cap for Edna & a new blue curtain for girls' room. Eli forgot to feed hens. He phoned Alice & she came up & gave them water. Her pay was all the eggs in nests (18).

Thursday, January 22, 1976. Mild weather continues. I burned trash & raked a little in front. Leah & Leanne were here in P.M. Jameses had gone to Kalona. Katie liked the little girls. She "talked" to them & stared at them from jumper.

Friday, January 23, 1976. Beautiful. No snow. Would be nice to have real winter again. Am writing while at dinner table. Hubby is gone. Baby lies awake in her bed. Heard her "talk" & squeak. Can hear clock ticking. 65 in P.M.

Saturday, January 24, 1976. Eli & I began cleaning dirty cistern. Removed slime, plastic glasses, a stick, & a toad, what remained! We didn't get done as he cleaned barn in P.M., etc. I ironed in evening and milked Marigold.

Sunday, January 25, 1976. Snow! Now it looks like winter. I've got a cold. We were at Paul Yoders for dinner. To ESFs for supper and singing.

Monday, January 26, 1976. Up & down the cellar steps carrying melted snow that was heated on gas stove. I washed diapers & baby clothes. Tried to make junket ice cream, but pudding turned sour. So I made another pudding & it was too thick. Wasn't really ice cream.

Tuesday, January 27, 1976. Katie went to Dr. Swenson for third time. She was very frisky on his table. He was well pleased with the head bones—they were loose. Sunny. I scrubbed chicken, beef, and pork jars in P.M.

Wednesday, January 28, 1976. Clock struck 10:30 & oh, my, what have I done since breakfast! Bathed & fed baby, scrubbed table cover, potted 6 plants & washed dishes. Must tend hens too & should sweep dirty floors. So tired by evening. Got the meat cans in place & sewed 2 baby pillow slips & quilting lining cover.

Thursday, January 29, 1976. There's a fox squirrel in our drive eating gravel bits. His body is in good shape but his tail seems rather thin this time of year. 12:25 P.M. Katie is dressed in a white dress & white bib after her bath. She's in her jumper now, contented. She "crowed" in bathroom this morning (more than a coo). 41 in P.M.

Friday, January 30, 1976. I made myself a cap but got the bottom taken across the material so made another 1. Didn't get the strings attached. Eyes did a lot of close work but baby slept well in my quietness.

Saturday, January 31, 1976. 2 robins are on the east side of house. 1 sat all puffed up on the snow. Eli hung out the wash. It began sprinkling in evening so diapers were a little damp. I baked a self-made cake with molasses & buttermilk & baked a loaf of bread.

Sunday, February 1, 1976. We attended church in southeast district at Abe Hochstetlers. Vernon Troyer of Buchanan County preached. Were to Pauls to see New Year baby.

Monday, February 2, 1976. Mom, Lois and Bertha came before I had my dirt cleaned up. They peeled apples, sliced & packaged ham & cut up squash. We "boppeld" [talked] most continuously. I canned squash in evening yet.

Tuesday, February 3, 1976. Katie rolled over from tummy to back for first time. Now she's holding both feet up & playing with the booties. I brought the remainder of our cabbage upstairs & canned 3 qt. squash.

Wednesday, February 4, 1976. Downtown we go early with Isaac Troyer. My Dad was yet in bed. Mom was up though. Eli went to ear tag [attach tags to the hogs' ears in order to identify them] & I took baby to doctor's office where Susie gave Katie her second DPT shot. Sewed at my folks & Mom patched men's socks for me.

Thursday, February 5, 1976. I finished Katie a bright yellow dress cut from a nightgown Bertha gave me that a woman she works for in Iowa City didn't want. Jamesport surprise guests were John Kings & Henry Fishers accompanied by Mrs. Peter T.

Friday, February 6, 1976. The teakettle was shined, rocking chair received a furry green cushion & back, baby a new cap, & dusting & sweeping were done. Jacob and Susan & Lloyds came in evening for apple snitzing [slicing]. We had soup & fritters for supper.

Saturday, February 7, 1976. Eli helped James work on the new barn. I went to Lawrence Rebecca's dry goods store & bought organdy, etc. Made Katie a white apron. Canned 14 qts. apples. Got to bed late.

Sunday, February 8, 1976. Beautiful sunset. Praise God for his loving kindness. He is so good. Were in church at ESFs.

Monday, February 9, 1976. Pretty sunrise. What meaneth the Lord? We have so much to be thankful for! I felt bum in morning. Couldn't pump water even up to 5 lbs. pressure. So I washed apple & squash jars & shelved them & sorted apples.

Tuesday, February 10, 1976. Eli rigged up the washing machine & carried water for me b-4 11:00 our time with some wash on the line. He came home with ice cream & a pair of brown jersey gloves for my birthday. Also gave me a hall tree!

Wednesday, February 11, 1976. 52 in A.M. Sunny & oh so nice. I shampooed my hair with hard water & soda & vinegar. I ironed and patched and slept so well in P.M. Katie pulls up her feet so agile-like.

Thursday, February 12, 1976. A nice morning. Lloyd Mae picked up "Missie Sunshine" and me. We went to ESPs for a quilting. Had good food. Very windy in P.M. Mom, Bertha, & Ann Marie were there, too.

Friday, February 13, 1976. Nice again. I washed out diapers & hung them up to dry. Held Missie for about 3 hours in A.M. Gave her cereal & honey water. Read from *Family Life* with her on my lap & talked to her about the "Gutmann" [God].

Saturday, February 14, 1976. Willie Ts, Ray & Lois, & our family went with Billy Stuzman in his long black 5 seat "limousine" to Princeton, Missouri, where we visited Earls. Had dinner in cafeteria style. Missie got her first taste of Dairy Queen on the way. She really liked it.

Sunday, February 15, 1976. [picture of sun shining] We attended gma [church] at Albert Troyers. Katie was fussy. Her teeth are bothering her. Is that why?

Monday, February 16, 1976. [picture of cloud and rain coming down] I gave Katie her first taste of squash diluted in milk. She liked it. I cut slits (from the hole out) in the cereal nipple. Then she drank better. It rained. I washed but didn't hang up all.

Tuesday, February 17, 1976. [picture of dark clouds] Foggy. We had fried mush, sorghum, & liverwurst for breakfast. Bill Bauf took me only to Iowa City. Dr. Sanders checked my eyes & found them improved! My new glasses are about double in price over my old ones. $82!! Whew, what a fortune.

Wednesday, February 18, 1976. [picture of cloud] I gave Katie her rattle balls to play with. She liked them & looked up at me from her crib & smiled. She's sleepy now & has thumb in her mouth—A.M.

Thursday, February 19, 1976. [picture of sun shining] I put "Missie Sunshine" in her high chair for the first time. Eli got it second-handed yesterday at Clifford Yoder's store in good condition. I baked bread & ironed. Made my black dress longer. Now it's longer, wider, & has a pocket.

Friday, February 20, 1976. [picture of sun shining] The friendly morning sun was rising as Eli set off for work about 7:00. However, by evening there was lightning and thunder. Rained a little. I wrote letters & got a package ready to send niece Lettie Yoder.

Saturday, February 21, 1976. [picture of snowman] Snowy & cloudy. We went to ESFs for dinner. Edna added fuel to the fire & the soot in the chimney started burning. Isaac got up on top of the roof & sent down chain [a technique for sweeping the chimney to remove soot buildup that could cause a chimney fire].

Sunday, February 22, 1976. We went to Lloyd B. Masts for dinner. Came home & chored, then to Elmers in evening.

Monday, February 23, 1976. [picture of sun shining] 68 in P.M. I didn't feel so peppy in morn so instead of starting the washing I began picking up the cover for Katie's bed. I replaced a better flannel. Made 2 bibs.

Tuesday, February 24, 1976. Was done washing before 10! Eli rigged up the machine & carried rinse water for me so that all helped. The wash dried nicely. I rested, then folded & put away wash.

Wednesday, February 25, 1976. Katie & I went to a quilting at Alice's house. Baby behaved well. Slept a good sleep. I enjoyed myself there. Some others present: Susan (Swartzendruber), Merle Lois, MAF, Bill F. Susan, & John Troyer Mary.

Thursday, February 26, 1976. [picture of sun shining] 75 in P.M. in sun. Katie & I went to Iowa City. I got a new pair of spectacles for $82!! (Bill Bauf took us). Katie sat in high chair in cow stable & watched me milk!

Friday, February 27, 1976. [picture of sun shining] What lovely weather! The maple tree south of house has fuzzy branches! And in Feb.! I brought in a twig & put it in water. Cleaned & prepared eats for supper. Had ham & peach pie with crumbs. ESFs were here, Lettie F., too.

Saturday, February 28, 1976. [picture of sun shining] Nice morn. Benny, neighbor's boy, was here to get milk & eggs. Since his mom had a birthday the other day, I asked him how old Alice is. He said, "78." I got a good laugh over that. He changed it to 38, though. I heard a mourning dove. The chickadee is calling "pee-wee!" So nice.

Sunday, February 29, 1976. We attended church at Peter Bontragers in the new house. Dads, Lois, & Charles Bender of Kansas were our supper guests. Mark & Erma were published to be wed.

January and February 1977

Saturday, January 1, 1977. Eli went to Jameses to help dress our beef from them. I washed chicken jars & toted them downstairs. We were at ESFs for dinner, then to Andy Ropps where we saw Elmers' baby Mae Betty. Was late when we got home.

Sunday, January 2, 1977. Church was at Albert Troyers for first time. I took Katie over to Josephs' house & got her to sleep. Fussy Little Miss. Amos Fisher & Michael B. Yoder preached. It snowed in A.M. Born to Larry Bs a Sarah today.

Monday, January 3, 1977. Jonah A. Fisher & Bertha came to get us to go to Busters to butcher. First we got our beef @ Jameses & left Katie there. We got a lot of hamburger and sold some in evening to Jacobs for 30 cents a lb. Joes, M. Annie, & Susan helped butcher.

Tuesday, January 4, 1977. Meat, meat—with James Rebecca's cooker & mine I canned over 40 qt. of meat and wrapped hamburger, plus put some in freezettes totaling 47 in all. Eli washed supper dishes. I picked bone meat.

Wednesday, January 5, 1977. More meat to can and can I did but less than yesterday. I mixed tenderquik and saltpeter [ingredients added to preserve meat], & salt to the bologna meat & returned it to the cold north porch to set until Friday. Eli cleaned walleyed pike (fish) in evening.

Thursday, January 6, 1977. Our kitchen floor is dirty. I can hardly stand it. After a mopping it's clean. I also made cracker jack and rice crispies candy, washed dishes, got ready & drove to Gingerich Implement for Eli. We went to Dan Brennemans.

Friday, January 7, 1977. Nice blue sky. I washed a big wash and hung out 60 diapers! I canned bologna after I mixed in the other ingredients. In evening we went to see Mom at the hospital. She has cancer. They operated on Tuesday.

Saturday, January 8, 1977. Cold and windy. Oh, yes, it would be nice to stay at home but after more bologna was canned & Eli hung up the remainder of wash, we headed for Joes to help b-4 they move to Missouri.

Sunday, January 9, 1977. Cold. Except when Eli went to Jameses with the milk we spent the day at home until the evening. ESFs came to take us along to hospital to see Mom. Grace Miller babysat for Katie & Fannie. Glen & Nelson were here too.

Monday, January 10, 1977. Cold. It takes a lot of fuel. I finished the morning chores for Eli after he'd left. Also ironed today. In evening Eli made good oatmeal cookies. Jacob Beilers of Missouri, Dad, Lois, & Bertha stopped in on way home from hospital.

Tuesday, January 11, 1977. Cold. Approximately 0/18. Mom is to have her second operation today. I made a big batch of noodles, mended clothes and canned 3 qt. of beef broth. Emma Jo was here to get eggs.

Wednesday, January 12, 1977. Wind from north. Very pretty blue sky. Not so cold in P.M. Katie really dedicated her what-had-been-new bedcovers by vomiting. The entire bed was stripped & quilt, comforter, & pad hung outdoors. I finished a pair of denims for Eli.

Thursday, January 13, 1977. Tired me. After writing Mom a letter I felt more rested. I also got a greeting card ready for her and finished a second pair of denim pants for Eli, buttons and all.

Friday, January 14, 1977. Merle Raber took me to Kalona. I had an appointment with Dr. Ballter [obstetrician]. Gained 1 1/2 lb. Katie walked beside me over the snow to Dads where we were for dinner. Mom returned home. Isn't well. Has spreading cancer.

Saturday, January 15, 1977. Eli finished Katie's high chair tray in A.M. We got to Joes late. Were there for dinner. In P.M. we had an auction among us to dispose of Joes' items outlawed in Missouri [items not allowed in the community where he was moving].

Sunday, January 16, 1977. Very cold. We had 0/23 in morn! We went to church at Albert Troyers. Small attendance. After church we went to Andy Ropps for dinner. Sam Millers, Mark Fs, Larry Benders, & Michael Ts were there.

Monday, January 17, 1977. I baked 7 loaves of bread, 18 rolls, and 70 Ranger cookies. In evening we ground beef bone meat & I mixed up a big batch of mincemeat yet.

Tuesday, January 18, 1977. Before breakfast 7 qt. of mincemeat were put in pressure cooker to can. I also canned sandwich meat in pints and washed. I hung out diapers. Dresses, shirts, etc. were hung in basement.

Wednesday, January 19, 1977. Merle Raber taxied me to Mark Fs where I helped Erma get ready for church. We washed Sunday dishes, cleaned part of basement and some worktable drawers. It snowed.

Thursday, January 20, 1977. Nice day. Not so cold. Pretty, pretty, blue sky. Katie discovered how to blow milk & water in a glass instead of drinking it. She blew water & laughed from the inside out! I ironed & folded wash.

Friday, January 21, 1977. I spent a lot of time cutting 2 more pairs of denim pants. I did a lot of piecing on the inside pieces in front. By evening I had sewn both pairs together. The sides & hems wait for finishing.

Saturday, January 22, 1977. Eli was at home. He went over figures & repaired a north porch window. I finished sewing the denim pants, made myself a slip, 2 pies, and cleaned in evening. After baths we retired.

Sunday, January 23, 1977. I rested well in bed after last eve's bath. We went to Jacobs for dinner. Had broiled sausage patties (good). MBFs, MABs, Ray & Lois & Joes were there, too, b-4 their move. Sang in P.M.

Monday, January 24, 1977. I cleaned commode drawers and arranged in it materials, gifts Katie had received, etc. Also readied a bureau drawer with infant garbs. I washed & hung out diapers. Earls stopped by in evening.

Tuesday, January 25, 1977. Eli took off in order to help Bills. They're loading today. We both helped. (Katie was left at Amos Fs). 24 people were there helping. Joes were here for supper & left @ about 1:30 A.M. for Missouri with Billie S.

Wednesday, January 26, 1977. Daddy got to bed late because he helped load up livestock until after midnight at Joes, last night. So I let him sleep later & milked the cow for him. Katie & I rested from A.M. In P.M. I ironed.

Thursday, January 27, 1977. Oh my, look out the window. The snow is really a-blowin'. Lois and Jacobs are coming home today from helping Joes move. Dangerous to be on road. I sewed another slip for myself & a dress for Katie of navy blue material from Levi Lapps.

Friday, January 28, 1977. A terrific northwest wind blasts into my face as I'm bringing in wood and robs breath from me. No public school. Drifts across roads. Hard to warm up living room in A.M. I did handwork (buttonholes & buttons).

Saturday, January 29, 1977. The oven baked 7 loaves of brown bread, and a batch of molasses cookies for me. Now wasn't that nice! Eli made oak wood & brought it in on a sled he made at Gingerich Implement today.

Sunday, January 30, 1977. We got to bed late and overslept late this morning. I bathed Katie & myself b-4 breakfast, stacked the dishes, & got ready for gma at Mark Fs. Sam Miller & Jerome preached.

Monday, January 31, 1977. And already the last day of Jan.! We're out of water so I can't wash very easily. Isaac T. took me to & from Dads. I was at Dr. Ballter's. Mom was restless in A.M. Had visitors today & yesterday.

Tuesday, February 1, 1977. Oh how pretty the weather. The "Miller the Driller" truck left us water in the cistern. I cut 4 small girls' flannel slips and a pink double knit baby dress, also pricked soil around potted plants.

Wednesday, February 2, 1977. Foggy. Snowed. After sewing 2 slips I began washing. Diapers & towels were hung out to be frozen & snowed on! In evening they were brought inside & hung up in living & dining rooms.

Thursday, February 3, 1977. Very nice (42 in P.M.). Thawing in A.M. Katie & I went outside in A.M. I gathered 25 eggs & gave the sheep water. Now I'm catching up my diary that Eli just bought last evening in Cedar Rapids!

Friday, February 4, 1977. Very windy but mild atmosphere. I put Katie in braids. Yesterday was the first time. I finished the fourth little slip & made a pink double knit baby dress.

Saturday, February 5, 1977. I did Saturday cleaning in kitchen & swept living room and bedrooms. Eli brought in a jag of firewood [an amount that will last a few days] with his tin toboggan & water tank. We took baths and went to Iowa City in P.M.

Sunday, February 6, 1977. 10 below 0 in morning. I helped with morning chores and trailed Eli to Jameses with the milk. In P.M. we saw baby Sarah at Larry Bs. In evening Mary Sue at James Bontragers. How little she is! We walked. Stars shone.

Monday, February 7, 1977. I baked soft white bread, rolls, & peanut butter cookies. In evening I started on the project of making baby announcements. To cut all the small diapers, make & address envelopes, etc. will require TIME.

Tuesday, February 8, 1977. I washed and hung out most of it. In P.M. Earl and Leonne stopped in to get 37 dozen eggs. They're on their way to Missouri to transport more of their possessions to Wisconsin. I ironed in evening.

Wednesday, February 9, 1977. Snow is melting. 68 in sun in P.M.! I did handwork on the pink double knit dressy and finished the announcements & envelopes for time being. Also made an everyday pair of blue thumbless mittens for Katie.

Thursday, February 10, 1977. Wet & dirty outdoors. 72 in P.M. in sun! Nice wedding day for Manford and Judith. I turned out the cow & horses, fed hens & got 20 eggs, burned trash, & gave Jameses' pigs our frozen Jonathan apples. My 35th birthday!

Friday, February 11, 1977. ESFs & Dan Brennemans were here last evening for my birthday. I was surprised. We had pizza & ice cream. Nice day. I lowered Katie's hems on her suit from Mom, resoled my house slippers, & made hard cinnamon candy.

Saturday, February 12, 1977. We had breakfast & dinner. In P.M. I fixed 2 doctor's gowns for nightgowns & patched a shirt for Eli. He cut and brought in wood with the wheelbarrow. Cloudy.

Sunday, February 13, 1977. We were at home from church. Nice day. Eli had great fun with Katie. I read from *Family Life*. In evening Eli took Katie to Lloyds. We stopped at Dads to see Mom. Went to hospital. Barbara was born.

Monday, February 14, 1977. I slept nothing at all last night & today that was real sleep. Am weak today. Eli came to visit me and gave me the details of happenings since last night. My roommate Betsy Newton has her second son.

Tuesday, February 15, 1977. I took a sitz bath & shower in A.M. After dinner I dressed & waited for Eli to come. He paid the hospital $297.90 & we left the hospital to go home with Barbara. Stopped at Dad's. Mom felt baby. See memo: Poor Mother is almost blind! Lies flat in bed with cancer [Sarah wrote this under the calendar's "Memoranda" section]. Bontragers & children, Joni Ws & Elmer were there, also Uncle Daniels. When we got home Edna, Leah, & Fannie were here. Eli left with Billy Mag to get Katie at Jacobs. In evening our family totaled 4! Leah is our hired girl.

Wednesday, February 16, 1977. Nice day. Leah made buns, rolls, & grapenuts. I had a grand surprise in P.M. Uncle Rays & Alberts, John Henry & Lydie, & Emma Mae called! Neighbors, Alice and Emma Jo called, too. Barbara is doing fine.

Thursday, February 17, 1977. I gave Barbara a bath & shampoo. Her hair is thick & wavy. Mae Annie stopped in to see the baby. I'm better today than yesterday. Leah washed. I braided Katie in 4 braids for my first time. Is cloudy in P.M.

Friday, February 18, 1977. Very nice today. I folded some wash, rested, and took care of baby. Leah ironed and raked. Baby is a big eater. She wants more than I can supply her with so I give her Similac. Katie held baby.

Saturday, February 19, 1977. In morning I bathed & nursed Barbara, combed Katie, & got myself ready to go to Dad's. Was tired by this time. At Grace's store I bought a pair of shoes, size 4 1/2 for

Katie. I read letters to Mom. Came home with our driver for dinner.

Sunday, February 20, 1977. Baby Barbara is a week old today. She weighs 7 lb. 14 1/2 oz. Hasn't regained birth weight. I weighed 147 lb. before breakfast. Dan Brenemanns were dinner guests. Had grapenut pudding—very good. ESFs, Larry Bs, Rachel & Rebecca—P.M. guests.

Monday, February 21, 1977. Quite windy. Leah washed. I washed dishes for second time now (last evening & this A.M.). I put Barbara in the infant seat for first time. She enjoyed it. Katie liked sitting tight beside me in rocker as I nursed baby.

Tuesday, February 22, 1977. Nice day—63. Leah ironed & made bread dough. I bathed Barbara and braided Katie. Also got baby greetings ready for the mail. Had pork 'n bean soup & fried eggs for supper.

Wednesday, February 23, 1977. "There shall be showers of blessing!" Rain in the morning and rain in the afternoon. Leah baked cookies and bread. I braided Katie and took care of baby. Had fresh apple pie & ice cream for supper.

Thursday, February 24, 1977. Leah left with Eli in morning. She went to Amos Ts to help ready for church. I finished breakfast dishes, got dinner & washed dinner dishes. Baby was very "brauf" [healthy]. Mother still lingers.

Friday, February 25, 1977. Cloudy and windy in morning. I started an answer to Mommy Hershberger's yesterday's letter. Leah finished Eli's chores in morning and washed diapers. Baby Barbara did well last night. She called me only once.

Saturday, February 26, 1977. Bontragers stopped in shortly. They now have moved to Buchanan County, Iowa, since Thursday. They went down to Dads. I helped with cleaning. Made Katie a cap and washed dishes after supper. Was tired.

Sunday, February 27, 1977. Leah & Katie went to church at Amos Ts & we to Dad's, all with Willie Yutzy. Mom is low. Poor Mother has to suffer so. Why? Lyn and Lettie, too, were there. David F. conducted prayers. Dan B. was there for supper.

Monday, February 28, 1977. Very pretty outdoors. 45 in P.M. in sun. Edna and Fannie were here in A.M. Isaacs went on to Iowa City with Thomas Yoder. Baby really cried in A.M. Leah washed and ironed. I rested, etc.

3 Sarah the Quilter: The Season of Quilting

Starting a marriage with four quilts is about right.
Four can keep the couple warm.
Sarah Fisher

Hungry to talk, Sarah and the other Amish women gather to quilt. Twelve inches of snow and low temperatures have kept Sarah and the children indoors. She hasn't talked face to face with anyone but her immediate family for a week or more. Letters and cards are diversions, but not enough.

AN INVITATION TO A QUILTING

THURSDAY, MARCH 12

SARAH FISHER'S

Sarah's postcard says it all. No need to state the time. Everyone knows the quilting begins at 10:00 A.M., includes a noontime dinner, and goes into the afternoon. No need to RSVP. Sarah knows that she will have a crowd, and the quilters know that they can come for any portion of the day to join in. Together, they'll produce a quilt, but more important, they'll hear one another's news. Their gathering is not unlike my book club. Sarah and her friends sew a quilt while I read a best-seller with my friends, but our needs and purposes are the same. We seek other women with whom to talk and so make sense of our lives.

Quiltings have always been a common part of Sarah's life, but I've had only one or two experiences with quilting. Three months before Stephen was born, I decided to make a baby's quilt out of a yellow and white small print with solid white alternating blocks. I quickly realized that the five days of spring vacation were not enough to complete the project, so out it went to the Bargain Basket Thrift Shop to be rescued by a more ambitious person than I. Several months later my Aunt Kate surprised me with a baby-sized quilt in a favorite pattern of mine, the Double Irish Chain.

Aunt Kate had also made a quilt for Steve and me as a wedding present in 1978. As a 4-H County Extension Coordinator for Eastern Iowa, she had had years of experience sewing and quilting. In her all-business manner, she handed me the neatly folded quilt and said, "Thought you might find this interesting." On a three-by-five card she had typed her summary:

REGARDING QUILT: Wild Goose Chase, a Bi-centennial pattern. Quilt top: recycled white shirts and blouses. Small blue print: recycled curtains. Filling: 100% Dacron Polyester Fiberfill. Back: cotton, cloth of gold. Size: 92 x 114 inches. Handquilted. Actual quilting time: 174 hours. Used 3 1/2 spools (250 yds. each or 875 yds.) quilting thread.

Aunt Kate made the quilt completely on her own, even scheduling in coffee breaks for herself at 10:00 and 2:00 each day. Through her gift, I learned what materials and time were necessary to complete such an undertaking, but I knew nothing about the process. I was soon to find out.

Inside the Season of Quilting

I was having supper at Sarah's. The dishes were cleared, and Sarah's niece, Lydia, a schoolteacher, generated, or pumped, the kerosene lantern to give a stronger light. She sat at the table marking the quilting pattern on the quilt top, the already pieced-together series of wool blocks. All the fabric came from Sarah's mother's dresses. The dresses were carefully taken apart, cleaned, and cut into the squares needed for the wall hanging. The edge was solid black, and hues of deep purple and forest green interplayed in the geometric pattern of one-inch wool squares making up the body. Lydia used chalk to mark a diamond pattern over the entire quilt top. Then she drew freehand feathers on the black border, a striking contrast to the strong geometrics.

Lydia explained, "Wall hangings sell better than quilts. They also take less time and materials to make." The wall hanging would not be displayed in an Amish home, since the Amish emphasis is on practicality and not on decoration. This Amish cottage industry, however, responds to the marketplace.

With all the questions I was asking, Sarah invited me to come the next day to her quilting. It was my chance to see how a quilt

Martha's Double Irish Chain.

Martha's Wild Goose Chase.

was put together, step by step. I walked up to the door of the three-and-a-half-story, gleaming white farmhouse. Stamping off my boots in the mudroom entrance, I stepped out of them and left them to dry. Even if I had been wearing clean, dry shoes, I would have felt compelled to take them off in deference to the sparkling, gray linoleum floor. I paused for a moment in the sunlight coming through the south windows, bright and white as it reflected off the walls, a welcome relief after the biting wind.

Sarah introduced me to those in attendance, her six sisters, each of whom had brought food. A sweet item, such as a cobbler or pie, is often served at a quilting, or even a complete dinner. This is determined by what is in season, but the decision is up to the hostess. Sarah pointed to the kitchen counter, which was filled with covered dishes. She had asked the others to bring a special, favorite dish from childhood for the refreshment time. Each sister talked about her dish and why it was a favorite. They all reminisced about their mother and their lives as little girls growing up. Sarah commented about changes in fabrics over the years: "My mother wore wool dresses. Nowadays, double-knit is used since it is so easy to care for. Using this fabric is very special for a quilt."

Unlike my Aunt Kate, who worked alone, Sarah's quilting group redistributes the workload from one to many pairs of hands. A quilt can thus be completed in a few days, as opposed to several weeks. Anna Swartz said that her sister-in-law quilts during March, April, and May, once each month, with four women on each side of the quilting frame. Two frames can be set up at one time, and the women may not be there for the completion of one entire quilt. They come and go, some attending one day, some more, rotating their chairs and positions.

Working as a group, Sarah and her sisters positioned the wall hanging top to be attached to the frame. One sister was in charge and, therefore, in control of the final decision on any question that might arise. Sarah explained this to me, and all the sisters smiled, hearing the humor in her voice. The positioning of the quilt top in the frame took about an hour.

Sarah said, "Do you think it should come this way?"

"I think so," said Edna.

"It looks crooked from this side. Stand over here where the light is better," said Sarah.

"I think you're right. Why did Lydia mark it this way?" asked Edna.

"Hand me the ruler." Four-year-old Rosetta left the couch where she was playing with her doll and handed a ruler to her aunt. She stood at eye level with the quilt frame. She looked at the quilt, then up at her aunt.

"Here, help me hold this, could you? It measures six inches from the edge here for the design. Try it on the other side," said Sarah. Rosetta helped her aunt hold the ruler and pull the fabric into place, young, smooth hands next to weathered ones.

"It is a quarter inch less on this side. We need to pull it this way," said Edna.

"Let's measure it one more time and then look," said Sarah.

In my brief foray into quilting I had read about this quilting approach in Safford and Bishop's *America's Quilts and Coverlets*. The fabric is cut into one-inch squares, or perhaps hexagons, and then sewn back together again into a specific pattern; the result is known as the patchwork quilt. Typically, Sarah pieces or patches fabric remnants together into the top of the quilt. When this is completed, a quilting pattern is marked on this cover with either chalk or motel-sized soap, which doesn't rub off as easily as chalk. Then a plain bottom piece of a coordinating color is sewn to the patchwork top. Finally, a filling is placed in between for warmth. Sarah said that polyester filling is preferred over the cotton batting used in years past because polyester doesn't shift or bunch together over time.

The three sandwiched pieces are then placed in the quilting frame to hold the cover taut during the quilting process. The frame is made of long, wooden poles with clamps on either end. The quilt is rolled tightly onto the wooden poles, and then unrolled a portion at a time so it is accessible from all four sides allowing many to quilt at once. The quilting pattern is sewn by hand with thread of either the same or a contrasting color as that of the fabric. The quilting pattern is made of tiny stitches, usually ten to an inch. It may follow the geometric shapes of the top or may be a complimentary pattern that adds interest, such as curved rows of stitching. The possibilities are endless.

All this took place at Sarah's in a sitting room off the kitchen, a room just large enough for the quilting frame and all the women. After about an hour, I became impatient. My curiosity about the quilting process was satisfied. The more I listened, the more it seemed that the talk stole time from the stitching. Who had seen the new neighbors? What were they like? Where were they from? How many cattle did they have? A recent funeral was discussed. Who had attended and what had been served? It looked like there would be a wedding soon in the Overholt family.

Then I felt guilty about my impatience. Everyone had been so kind; I had even been offered a place at the quilting frame. And as I listened and stitched, I thought of my book group. Though our discussions center on interpretations of characters' motives, what the author really meant, or what would happen next if the author had kept writing, we often abandon the book altogether and talk of daily frustrations at work, the best computer to buy, sick relatives, or the good news about our children's latest accomplishments. I realized that the talk was more important than the stitching or production of a quilt, just as the time my book club spends discussing life's disappointments and victories is what is crucial, not the book.

Sarah and I interpret our lives in relation to the stories of others. Instead of interpreting a written text as I do in my book group, Sarah and her friends speculate upon the text of their daily lives, the stories of the people in their community.

Sarah's quilting-group discussions seemed significant, because I knew that her community favors a practical, straightforward approach to life and does not encourage speculation and interpretation of the written word or of conversation. But I saw that interpretation of events and life's circumstances was taking place in the talk around Sarah's quilting frame. I also found her artistic voice in her diary, as I read her accounts of sewing pajamas for her daughter out of fabric remnants and of collaborating with husband Eli on a waffle supper to conclude a quilting.

On a later visit after the quilting, when I told Sarah that her group reminded me of my book club, she asked me what we read. I started to describe a recent selection, Dennis Covington's *Salvation on Sand Mountain: Snake Handling and Redemption in Southern Appalachia*, but stopped. Best-sellers are not allowed in Sarah's community. Sarah and Eli carefully monitor their books and magazines for consonance with their religious beliefs. They read publications such as *Family Life*, written by and for the Amish with short stories that reflect biblical morals and lessons.

I try at all times to remind myself that I am a visitor, a temporary participant, an outsider. Perhaps our friendship exists because of it. I need to be very careful; I sense that she tries to be, too. Once while reading aloud a letter from an Amish friend in Wisconsin, she stopped partway through the closing, "God's blessings upon you" and a Bible verse. She said, "Well, we're from different worlds. Anyway, you can see what she's doing in her garden from the letter." I thanked her and asked if I could help shell the rest of the peas.

Sarah's Attic Quilt Cache

I wondered about the quilts Sarah had stored in her attic. Were some the ones with which she had begun housekeeping as a married woman? Did she still have the child's quilt she mentioned in the diary? We went to her attic storage, and Sarah pulled out quilt after quilt.

"You get quiltpox. It comes with age," Sarah said. She explained that many older women have more time to quilt because their children are grown, and quilting grows on a person. Although Sarah likes to quilt, she doesn't have time to quilt extensively at this point in her life, and she has many to finish. We spread them out to look at the patterns.

For me, quilts are decorative, but Sarah's purpose is practical. Her quilts are bed coverings for use in a house heated only by a central wood-fueled stove. I asked Sarah about the Amish rule I had heard: "Four quilts for each child before leaving home." She said, "Starting a marriage with four is about right. Four quilts can keep the couple warm." Bedrooms are quite cold during the winter, and several quilts are a necessity. One young woman had pieced together twenty-one quilts by the time she left home. The same woman's husband brought two to their marriage. Sarah added that Eli had a Tumbling Block and Lone Star before they were married.

Sarah said she developed her interest when she helped her mother quilt the pattern called Grandmother's Flower Garden. Sarah's mother found it easier to store quilt tops than an entire quilt, so if a work was in progress, the top was stored until there was time to finish it. She laughed, "Now I have my mother's Grandmother's Flower Garden, and I have to finish it." The pattern begins in the center and radiates outward with hexagon blocks, every piece a different color. Sarah said, "There's always something that needs to be finished in the way of quilting. There must be one thousand blocks here!"

Sarah went on to say the following:

The quilts in our community are changing. Now they're more colorful compared to when I was married. Then they were pink and

Sarah's Lone Star.

Sarah's Plain Top.

white; now the darker tones are more desired. As I plan to do more quilts, I think I'd now like to do more than one kind. I'd like to do a plain top where you have your own choice of color, then create a scene on the top. There's no limit. You can make any scene you want. One that Eli had before our marriage was a plain top with a deer stitched on the top. I liked it so well that I made one up. I was walking in the timber, found some oak leaves, and then used them as patterns for my plain top design. I had the quilting frame set up and used tan with sateen fabric. I don't know that anyone has used this design idea. I also think diamonds are easy and add to the appearance of a quilt.

I found the term "plain top" to be a misnomer. All Sarah's quilts are more complex when examined closely than they seem at first glance. The Tumbling Block, with varying shades of blue and an aqua border, created an optical illusion I didn't notice until Sarah asked, "Can you see it tumbling?" Indeed, I could.

For Amish women, the months of March and April are commonly the quilting months. In reading Sarah's diary entry for December 9, 1976, I feel her excitement to see company: "Mother Goose hustled & bustled about to get ready for her party. She cooked & cleaned & put a child's quilt in frame. When all was ready the neighbors came, Mary Bertha & children (minus William), Amoses & Samuels. We had a waffle supper, quilting bee & popcorn shelling."

At the end of my quilting day with Sarah, I drove home, unlocked the door, walked into the pantry, and pressed the play button on my phone message recorder. Excitement replaced my fatigue as I heard Julie's voice: "I'll pick you up at 6:45 for Book Club!" I couldn't wait for the talk.

Sarah Fisher's Recipes for a Quilting

WAFFLES

Sarah serves waffles with her home-processed molasses and butter, her own applesauce cooked from fresh apples stored in her basement, and coffee.

2 cups flour
3 tsp. sugar
3 tsp. baking powder
1/2 tsp. salt
1 and 3/4 cups milk
2 eggs (separated)
4 tablespoons butter

Sift dry ingredients together. Add the egg yolks and milk slowly. Beat until smooth. Then add the melted butter and stiffly beaten egg whites. Pour into waffle griddle on top of cookstove.

APPLESAUCE

Sarah said, "I'm guessing on this one, as I never measure anything."

Cook an apple that goes into sauce, Transparent, Wealthy or such. Add just enough water to come up 1/3 of the way on the apples. Boil until well done. Rub through a sieve or colander. Add sugar to taste, and a small sprinkle of salt. Good eating.

CHERRY COBBLER

For a lighter refreshment during an afternoon quilting, Sarah serves her guests cherry cobbler and Folger's coffee.

1 egg
1 cup sugar
1 and 1/2 cups cherries
1 and 1/2 cups flour
1/4 tsp. salt
1 level tsp. soda

Mix well and bake at 350 degrees in a 9 x 9 pan for 25 to 30 minutes.

CHERRY PUDDING

1/2 cup sugar
1/4 cup shortening
1 egg beaten
1 cup flour
1 tsp. soda dissolved in 2 tsp. water
1 cup cherries and juice
1/2 tsp. cinnamon

Combine ingredients in order given and mix well. Pour into a 9 x 9 pan. Bake in a 350-degree. oven for 25 to 30 minutes.

MARTHA'S DESSERTS FOR BOOK CLUB

For evening book club, I serve several coffee choices and low-fat desserts, such as angelfood cake made from a boxed mix. I find fresh fruit also takes little time. Whole strawberries, sliced pears sprinkled with cinnamon and served with nonfat cream cheese, and grapes combine well with the cake and decaffeinated hazelnut, French roast, and raspberry creme coffees. I smiled when I read Sarah's diary entry of March 9, 1976: "I baked an angelfood cake with success. My highest yet." (Sarah does not use boxed mixes to save time.)

March and April 1976

Monday, March 1, 1976. I tried my luck in making brown bread. It worked. Also baked applesauce cookies and pluckits [dough rolled into balls and baked in a casserole dish with sugar and cream on top; you "pluck" a ball out of the dish to eat it]. I painted flowers on the diaper pail & lid. It was a dreary day.

Tuesday, March 2, 1976. [picture of dark clouds] Foggy. While washing clothes downstairs, Joe knocked at the door. He had brought Vera & the children. He went to the sale at Jacob Yoders. Vera & I marked off quilt & talked!

Wednesday, March 3, 1976. [picture of cloud] Still cloudy & overcast. I hung up the remainder of wash. Gave "Missie" a bath. She likes them. Enjoys the feel of the warm water. In P.M. I cut and sewed her a yellow dress for the wedding.

Thursday, March 4, 1976. [picture of cloud with lightning] Rainy, lightning & thunder. Icy trees. Our maple tree was an unusual sight. Its "blossoms" were coated with ice & icicles hung from the branches. Amidst the rain & thunder I went to Pops with baby! We quilted.

Friday, March 5, 1976. [picture of cloud with face "blowing" wind] Overcast & windy. Eli rode our new colt to work. I watched him go. She galloped up the hill going fine. In evening he came home very disgusted. Even broke his new plastic dinner pail!

Saturday, March 6, 1976. Eli Fisher, my husband, was "molendlich" [at home]. He made a small shelf for above sink & fixed a hook for chicken house door. I sewed button holes & hemmed up Missie's yellow suit. First suit for her. Made chocolate cake & apple pie & pumpkin custard.

Sunday, March 7, 1976. We were at home in A.M. Went to a farewell singing for Paul Gingerich in P.M.

Monday, March 8, 1976. I took Katie & went to Jeromes with Shorty. Helped bake angelfood cake & raked. Fed Katie from baby food grinder for first time. She made a face over the mixture of potatoes, beans, & seasoned meat. Almost gagged.

Tuesday, March 9, 1976. Sale today at Paul Gingeriches. We didn't go. They're leaving for Wisconsin Thursday. I baked an angelfood cake with success. My highest yet. Washed clothes. Also washed off buggy.

Wednesday, March 10, 1976. I returned the blankets to Willie Mary & Ben Emma Joe that they had given me to use. Swept kitchen & shook rugs. I ironed in P.M. Helped chore in evening. I carried milk to Jameses instead of husband doing it.

Thursday, March 11, 1976. For breakfast Katie had her first taste of egg yolk. We attended Mark & Erma's wedding. Ceremony at Fred Benders. I was cook. Sunny in A.M. Windy in P.M. Rained after dark. Had a nice wedding for most part. "Bellers" [persons not invited to the evening dinner] & made noise. Nonsense!

Friday, March 12, 1976. Leanne & Irma Bontrager were here while Jameses helped James Bontrager move from Mast place to Jacob Yoder's place. It rained in P.M. I baked cherry & pumpkin pies, 1 of each.

Saturday, March 13, 1976. We baked crispy oatmeal cookies— 3 batches. *Went to Paul Fisher's sale.* This was written with Mama's hand over Missie's patty! (ha) Charles Yoder & J. James auctioneered.

Sunday, March 14, 1976. Church at Peter Bontragers. F. F. Yoder had main sermon. Andy Lapps of Missouri were there. We went to Lloyds for supper. Had chili soup.

Monday, March 15, 1976. Nice wash day. Lots of diapers. I used wash water to scrub buggy. Also scrubbed porch floor & washed off cellar steps. We went to Dr. Betz in Cedar Rapids.

Tuesday, March 16, 1976. [picture of sun shining] I folded wash & ironed. Read from New Testament & *Family Life* & became quite involved in Gurney's Seed Catalogue. My gardening spirits soared. Macaroni chicken, eggs, chocolate milk, pork 'n beans for supper tonight. It's ready. Hubby's out.

Wednesday, March 17, 1976. Nice day. I took a bath & shampooed my hair, finished the dress for Katie that Mom had begun & gave me before it was done. Also fixed the green dress Mae gave for baby. It's not done yet. And mended clothes. Bye—

Thursday, March 18, 1976. Katie & I went to a quilting @ FBM Jrs. Mom had my quilt in frame. I took Emmanuel Leah along. Joseph Fisher's funeral was today. He died Tuesday. Jonah Clara & Rachel were the others present @ the quilting.

Friday, March 19, 1976. Before breakfast I rolled out pie dough & stuck 4 or 5 pumpkin pies in the oven. Then we went over to James Bontragers. Eli carried baby through the "bush" [the woods between the properties] & I the pies. I helped Rebecca put up the meat. Went barefoot.

Saturday, March 20, 1976. Mark and Erma moved today & Jeromes, too. Small children carried canned goods from big cellar to little house. We got home late. Marks were moved better in house by evening than Jeromes were.

Sunday, March 21, 1976. We were at home all day (except for hubby's trip to neighbors to carry milk). First time since Sunday School closed. Missie was so lively. Even after 9 she wasn't asleep!

Monday, March 22, 1976. 'Twas bake day in the Fisher Kitchen [some years later she started a baking business named the Fisher Kitchens]. The Mrs. [Sarah herself] turned out bread, rolls, ground cherry pies, apple jello, and potato salad. Then I had all the dishes to wash and so many!

Tuesday, March 23, 1976. The south wind blew lively & really shook the wash a-flying on the line. I took down dry clothes before the wash was all hung up! In P.M. I mended & folded clothes. Made 3 bibs today.

Wednesday, March 24, 1976. I have a head cold. Didn't feel very peppy at breakfast time. Afterwards I fixed 5 lunches. Picked up Emmanuel Leah & went visiting schools: Oak Grove, Brookside, and Meadowview [named after the geographic attributes of their locations]. I took Glen and Nelson's lunches. They didn't know who would furnish them [a kind deed like this, provided unexpectedly, is a frequent Amish gesture].

Thursday, March 25, 1976. My cold's better. I got a cold by going barefoot last Friday! Leah & the girls were here. Wanda made noodles & angelfood cake, Mom trimmed grapevines & baked grapenuts & ironed, & Leah ironed. I supervised.

Friday, March 26, 1976. Rainy. I sewed 2 seed bags for use in planting garden, mended, and made 2 cheesecloth covers for milk pails.

Saturday, March 27, 1976. A pretty P.M.—sunny but cool. Daddy [Eli] is having fun from the inside out. He's flying a kite and has 3 rolls of plastic coated cord knotted together making 250 feet. Now he's got the last ball of cord & total length is 1000 feet. I'm piecing a baby quilt—Tumbling Block. Baby is brauf. Baby had her first fall this morning.

Sunday, March 28, 1976. Went to gma @ Emil & MAFs. Lloyd B. & David preached. We went to Ephriam Yoders to see baby in P.M.

Monday, March 29, 1976. I washed. Was cloudy. Hung some wash outdoors & other clothes downstairs. We left some out overnight & guess what! It rained. I sewed further on my tumbling block quilt for baby bed.

Tuesday, March 30, 1976. I ironed & brought in rain-washed clothes, baked an angelfood cake & gave it to Elmers in evening. He had his second leg operation last Wednesday and came home yesterday. Wilson Yoder is helping with chores.

Wednesday, March 31, 1976. Very nice outdoors. I took our coated frying pan outdoors & gave it a scratching off which was much needed. It had been used by another who didn't wash it right & grease built up. Picked up aprons & remade 1 and part of another.

Thursday, April 1, 1976. Katie & I went to a Sarah quilting [quilters named Sarah convened to quilt] @ Andrew Yoders. Andrew Sarah gave us a candy jar (glass) for remembrance [a gift by which to be remembered, a party favor]. In evening I stopped @ Bill Claras. Got a large roaster & aluminum dish pan, material & quilt batting.

Friday, April 2, 1976. Diapers were hand washed & hung out, 3 pies & 1 cake baked, my head shampooed, 2 pillow slips made, & started making new curtains for bedroom. In P.M. Sam Rebecca & Edna stopped in. Edna brought us grapevines & planted them. We attended a singing @ Cottonwood Grove in evening.

Saturday, April 3, 1976. Our family went on a route. At Grace's store we purchased groceries & new black shoes for Katie, size 3. Stopped @ ESFs for a gallon paint, then to Marks & Bill Clara, on to Kalona. Were at FBM Jrs for dinner. I made baby a light blanket with Bertha's sewing machine. Came home at chore time.

Sunday, April 4, 1976. We went to first day of Sunday School. Attendance was 98. James Bontrager was elected teacher. In P.M. we viewed the corpse of Lydie Stolzfus and visited Charles Elizabeth who had a light stroke.

Monday, April 5, 1976. Last evening I nursed baby yet for the last time. She was 6 months old yesterday. Nice morning. Will have tomato gravy & egg dutch [scrambled eggs made with eggs and cream or milk] for breakfast. I washed & folded wash, painted the teeter babe & grapevine posts. Bontragers came in evening. (We planted peas in evening).

Tuesday, April 6, 1976. In morning I made apple jello salad & cooked macaroni & eggs for salad, planted peas, bathed baby, hitched Blackie to buggy & rode to Elmers. They had a frolic [a gathering of many to accomplish a specific task] to put in fence. Womenfolk prepared dinner & did house cleaning.

Wednesday, April 7, 1976. I grouped canned goods in cellar, made a path in the garden, & planted lettuce, radishes, & carrots. Also baked 6 loaves of bread. We had supper at Elmers in honor of Bontragers. They were our overnight guests.

Thursday, April 8, 1976. Beautiful morning. Eli left for work. Elmers drove to Dads with Perry and buggy in A.M. Mae dressed baby in the morning. I planted carrots, spinach, radishes, kohlrabi, & bush beans.

Friday, April 9, 1976. To Joes to help get ready for gma went Mother & Katie. Emmanuel & Hattie & Hebert & Ann, too, were there. We baked, sewed, & raked. I bought a 10 gallon milk can & 1 gallon fish oil from Lloyd Helmuth in evening. We went to Brookside School singing in evening.

Saturday, April 10, 1976. I sewed 2 small pillow slips, hemmed the baby bedspread from Bill Clara (green), hung out diapers, ironed, hemmed up Katie's green dress from Mae and refixed my white cap. Katie was along out this P.M. when Eli began sawing up the old corncrib.

Sunday, April 11, 1976. We were to gma at Neal & ERS. Was Council meeting. Went to Joes in evening for the singing.

Monday, April 12, 1976. I sat down & made "Missie" a white cap but it wasn't to my appeal so I cut a pattern from a hood Edna gave me that had been a liner for Eli and tried again. I made a pink cap or hood. It's nice but too short. I washed & folded wash.

Tuesday, April 13, 1976. Eli and I planted potatoes before breakfast (the Red Chieftain). I raked and made Katie a brown hood from a "halsduch" [a garment that fits over the top of a dress from the waist up] remains. An Indian (Cherokee) stopped in with herbs [a Cherokee woman who sells herbs visits Sarah's community every year].

Wednesday, April 14, 1976. Early, by 4:00, I was up. After dressing I began ironing. In A.M. I marked off the baby quilt. Cleaned fruit room for the time being & did house cleaning up on main floor. We went to Fellowship School singing in evening.

Thursday, April 15, 1976. I put 2 coconut custard pies and a Wacky cake & pumpkin custard in oven before breakfast. Made pineapple jello salad and hurried with dishes. Had a quilting. Dads, Ann, Faye, Susan were here. I bought herbs from the Indian woman.

Friday, April 16, 1976. Eli told me my peas were up and I didn't even know it. After dinner I was surprised to find my radishes, too, were up & lettuce was up also. How good for such little rain since I sowed them last week. Is nice to have husband at home today.

Saturday, April 17, 1976. We had an appreciated rain last night. My cabbage is up now, too. Very windy & cloudy. I'm quilting by myself on the baby quilt. A spring bouquet of bluebells & narcissus & 1 daffodil dominate the center of the table. Eli went to Henry Fishers to help on the Fred Fisher Grandpa house [a small house for the grandparents of the household, built adjacent to the large farmhouse].

Sunday, April 18, 1976. Were at Sunday School, home for dinner. In evening we toured west cemetery.

Monday, April 19, 1976. Eli hung out the wash & I washed. We were done by a little after 8:00 A.M. We ate breakfast then & got ready to go bye. Were at Ned Yoders for dinner. Baby was fussy. Maybe she had earache from overexposure last evening.

Tuesday, April 20, 1976. Baby had a fever today, but slept well in P.M. I gave her pain reliever. We bathed her in vinegar & soda water & gave her an enema. I finished quilting the baby quilt & folded wash. Cloudy & rainy. Was glad I washed yesterday.

Wednesday, April 21, 1976. Our dwarf apple tree is bursting with lovely blooms. I cut various clothes items and sewed for Kenny Don a yellow hood & dress & kimono [baby clothing]. Started

2 white hoods for Missie. She sat up well today. Fell over twice in bed.

Thursday, April 22, 1976. Pancakes for breakfast. It rained a little b-4 7. Soil is well saturated. Eli had a rogue of a time in getting off for work with rebellious Minnie [the horse]. I was out & helped in my feminine weakness! She was more subdued, but husband was pooped out!

Friday, April 23, 1976. Rain again. Surely was a good thing we washed Monday as it was rainy every day since or mostly so. The sun did shine though yesterday P.M. when I hung up diapers. I baked bread successfully & sewed 2 everyday aprons. Missie was fussy in A.M. but slept well in P.M.

Saturday, April 24, 1976. Yesterday I sat baby on an old quilt on the floor & Thursday, too. She can sit alone but tumbles yet. She enjoys sitting by herself. I made myself 2 night slips. Eli was at home for dinner. He put "Vieh" [cow] to pasture along roadside.

Sunday, April 25, 1976. Church began on fast time [Daylight Savings Time]. Had communion at Michael Bs. We visited William Fs & Brother Jacobs in P.M. Saw Kenny Don for first time. It snowed.

Monday, April 26, 1976. A nice wash day. It was done washing in less than 2 hours. It went well. In evening we ate first before Eli chored. We began knitting baby's comforter & Eli read the family letter [a circle letter passed among family members]. Baby & I really had fun. We really laughed. I copied her sounds, and she laughed more than ever b-4.

Tuesday, April 27, 1976. Damp & cloudy in morning. The newlyweds were here to invite us to their wedding May 6—Mark and Elsie Ann. My dishes weren't washed yet. Katie likes pickles. I gave her 1 & she chewed & sucked on it. Good for her gums, too.

Wednesday, April 28, 1976. Old Marigold got out of her roadside pasture. She escaped into the north timber & I couldn't get her!

I began sewing even before I was married.
—Sarah Fisher

Marvin Yoder's boy found her on the road or somewhere & tied her up. I made Katie a blue bonnet.

Thursday, April 29, 1976. I put together a white Sunday hood for Katie of double knit & white smooth lining, made black everyday suspenders, patched baby pants, sewed buttonholes, button, & snaps, & mowed grass. Spaded some between grapes & raspberries.

Friday, April 30, 1976. I wanted to spade in garden in morning. Now it's raining after breakfast & I didn't get out b-4 eating. Spaded after all for 1 1/4 hour in A.M. Trimmed along walks, washed diapers by hand, & made Katie a Sunday cap.

March and April 1977

Tuesday, March 1, 1977. Joes stopped in to see the baby. They came Sunday evening and returned home today. I wrote 2 letters, cared for baby & rested. Leah raked in ditch & on bank. Katie was outdoors, too. Chilly wind but pretty day.

Wednesday, March 2, 1977. Isaac T. took Leah, my daughters, & me to Dads. Sister Lyn & Lettie are there yet helping along. Mom is a sick person but complains little or none. Leah learned how to macrame from Lois. Lois gave me one.

Thursday, March 3, 1977. Cloudy. A rain puddle stands in road. Katie likes her sister, but cannot be fully trusted when she sticks her finger in the baby bed. Katie really gets around. On the run is she.

Friday, March 4, 1977. Cloudy. Leah washed diapers, baby blankets, & kimonos. I assembled *Young Companions*, took care of baby & helped make supper, also folded diapers. Had vegetable-chicken with dumplings.

Saturday, March 5, 1977. Leah cleaned. Eli finished cleaning the fencerow of young trees east of driveway. I rested. Very nice out. Baby was brauf. Katie was a real busybody. She unraveled toilet tissue.

Sunday, March 6, 1977. Emmanuel Johns came to see baby Barbara before we were ready. They came early, then went to James Bs for dinner. Lloyds were our dinner guests. In P.M. Isaac Helmuths, Wilbur Ss & Willie Fs came. Had meatloaf & mince pie for dinner.

Monday, March 7, 1977. Eli rode Brownie horseback all the way to Kalona Sale Barn to sell her. He went on up to Dads to see how Mom was, but she had passed away about 2:30 A.M. We went down in P.M. Were there for supper.

Tuesday, March 8, 1977. Eli is not working this week until after the funeral. We & baby drove down to Dads in A.M. Were there for dinner, then went up to homeplace in P.M. Mother's body came out, too, in P.M. Nice day.

Wednesday, March 9, 1977. Nice day. We went up to homeplace. Bontragers, Joes, & Earls arrived as well as other relatives & friends out-of-state. Young folks sang in evening [a common practice at the prayer service or wake the night before a funeral]. I was very, very tired. Went upstairs & rested in wake time.

Thursday, March 10, 1977. Our family attended the funeral in A.M. Many strangers were present. Attendance of funeral about 500 [a number that is typical]. Both houses were used. Mother was laid to rest in cemetery leaving loved ones behind in sorrow.

Friday, March 11, 1977. Eli returned to work. It rained. We needed moisture. Alice [a non-Amish neighbor] brought us a Hawaiian pineapple from their trip. I felt more rested this morning than yesterday morning. Rested today, too.

Saturday, March 12, 1977. Ina and I prepared eats for Sunday dinner. We cleaned in P.M. Eli took Leah to Charles Benders for the night. She wants to go to church tomorrow at Elwin Yoders.

Sunday, March 13, 1977. Eli went to church at Amos Ts. Fred & Leah, Mark & Erma were here for dinner. We had chili soup, potato salad, apple jello, ice cream & pie. Had more visitors today than other Sundays. 8 households.

Monday, March 14, 1977. Nice day. A swift breeze which set the wash on the line a-fluttering. I made all 3 meals & washed the dishes afterwards, too. Feel pretty good today. We sorted popcorn in evening.

Tuesday, March 15, 1977. I feel tired this morning. Had a long day yesterday. Baby didn't settle down until 10–10:30. Cloudy & windy. Sisters Lyn, Lois, & Bertha were here for dinner. They went to visit Emmanuel Leah from here.

Wednesday, March 16, 1977. 67 in sun in P.M. Very beautiful spring P.M. Leah raked ditch & bank north of garden. I marked hankies of mine. Katie likes to play with kitchen tools better than her toys, also leftover containers.

Thursday, March 17, 1977. Rainy. Isaac T. took me to Kalona. Lyn is still at EFM. We sorted Mom's clothing. I got her rubbers, shawl, organdy, dresses, etc. Katie stayed home with Leah. I put sweet potatoes in water.

Friday, March 18, 1977. In A.M. I washed and ironed caps and lady's white apron. Leah washed woodwork in kitchen. Had chicken & sweet potatoes for supper. Eli went to Grace's store in evening.

Saturday, March 19, 1977. Leah washed down the living room ceiling & walls. Eli went to Lloyds to help with woodworking in house. I prepared cinnamon pudding, pies, cake, & graham cracker fluff.

Sunday, March 20, 1977. Elmers & Jacobs were here for dinner & Sam Ms & Willie Js, Chesters, Sam Millers & girls & Andy Ropps in P.M. For supper—William Fishers of Kansas. Dad & girls & MABs, MBFs, BJMs. I enjoyed having supper company.

Monday, March 21, 1977. It really snowed. Leah did the washing. I ate a late breakfast.

Tuesday, March 22, 1977. Leah hung out wash & washed down the wash room. I pulled 10 white hairs from my head! (ha). Katie was more contented today than at most other times. She said "Katie" for the first time.

Wednesday, March 23, 1977. After the chilly wind died down weather was very nice. Snow is melting fast. We went to Glen Helmuths in evening to help get ready for gma. I made pies.

Thursday, March 24, 1977. Baby is 5 weeks old and smiles. Ina began piecing a baby quilt of white & purple. I bathed & rested in P.M. Leah and Eli pruned grapevines in evening. Teacher Dorothy Lapp visited.

Friday, March 25, 1977. Leah washed diapers & pieced quilt. My bread turned out very successfully, but my rolls separated some—too loose dough. We went to Lloyds to prepare for gma in evening. Isaac Helmuth took us.

Saturday, March 26, 1977. Leah got up in morning & out of the house while we slept. She milked Marigold. How kind! She also washed down Katie's room & pieced quilt. I made pumpkin bars and apple custard pie. Eli took Leah home & Katie along where she stayed for over Sunday.

Sunday, March 27, 1977. We had [church] council meeting at Evan Yoders. Eli had an infection in his hand so we stayed home. He bathes it a lot. We ate twice & slept. I milked Marigold in morning but he did in evening.

Monday, March 28, 1977. Rainy day. Leah returned with ESFs' rig [buggy] bringing Katie along home. We left her sitting on the seat with slide [the door on the side of the buggy; operates like a window shade] open & she fell out getting her clothes black with grease. Leah washed. Barbara got blue material from Jeremiah Erma so I started a bonnet from it.

Tuesday, March 29, 1977. Grass has really greened up! Windy in A.M. Sunny from morning till now at 2 P.M. Baby is fed & relaxing on sofa. She watched the pendulum [on the wall clock] swing. I finished the bonnet. Katie may wear it this summer & Barbara next year Lord willing.

Wednesday, March 30, 1977. Daughters & I went to Dr. Swenson in Cedar Rapids. Baby was all right, but Katie & I were tight [in need of chiropractic treatment]. Eli saw a mouse while washing supper dishes.

Thursday, March 31, 1977. Until babies were clothed & fed, Katie & I combed, firewood brought in & fire started, breakfast dishes & milk pails washed, it was close to 11:30! Cloudy (A.M.). We had twin lambs in morning. Sister Mae stopped in P.M. Surprised me.

In evening we planted 75 strawberry plants. Memo: I also planted 1 clump of Canada Red Rhubarb at the east end of the black raspberries south row—April 1 [Sarah wrote this note in the memorandum portion of the calendar].

Friday, April 1, 1977. Windy & cloudy. Willie Lois took my girls & me to MCY for a quilting. Mrs. ESF, Wanda, & Leah, Marvin Betty, & Susan Ella, too, were present. In evening I planted a clump of Canada Red rhubarb plants.

Saturday, April 2, 1977. Before breakfast I washed 2 batches of diapers. In A.M. washed the buggy with wash water. Made a light blue bonnet for Barbara in P.M. Eli hauled manure from pile, barn & henhouse.

Sunday, April 3, 1977. Sunday School opened again. Election cast Al Beiler as teacher, Brother Jacob to be secretary. Attendance was 131. Changes present since last year: 4 babes, 1 newlywed couple, lost 2 households. Uncle Rays & Alberts, FBM & girls, & we marrieds were at MAB for supper.

Monday, April 4, 1977. Katie is now 1 and 1/2 years old. It really snowed in A.M. What a pretty scene it made. I baked 7 loaves of bread, 2 pans of rolls, 3 pans of "steeper" [coffee cake made from one piece of yeast dough and baked with cinnamon, sugar, and cream over the top] & made a few cookies & ginger cremes (bars).

Tuesday, April 5, 1977. Very windy. It snowed briefly in P.M. I washed, ironed, & folded & put away clothes. Willie Alice brought us 2 large Florida-grown pineapples. Baby was good.

Wednesday, April 6, 1977. Pretty day. I gave Katie a wagon ride across Jameses' small pasture east of house. Began removing black paint from the chest of drawers we got recently. We slept in P.M.

Thursday, April 7, 1977. What a Mrs. Hurry in the house this morning! Swept & mopped in the living room & kitchen before Isaac T. came to take my daughters & me to Dad & Bertha's. Came home with Ben M. in evening. Nice day.

Friday, April 8, 1977. Good Friday. We had "fast tag" [a fast day in which no breakfast is eaten and time is spent in Bible reading and prayer]. In P.M. Elmer Ropps came to see baby. We went to Mark Millers for supper. ESFs came, too, before we were done eating. Born today 2 girls for Dale (Irma) & Willis (Anna Mary) F.

Saturday, April 9, 1977. I washed diapers and some other clothes. Was tired by P.M. Eli trimmed our dwarf apple & peach trees and cleaned the stable for our young folks' company tomorrow night (5 couples).

Sunday, April 10, 1977. Our communion services were held at Evan Yoders. Katie did fine on Daddy's lap in A.M. Was a little more fussy in P.M. Baby slept well on Mama's lap. Sunny. South breeze. Andy B. visiting minister.

Monday, April 11, 1977. Very warm south wind. 90 in shade at 12:45. Babes are sleeping. Husband & I lunched, then he left for work. It's Easter Monday. We had 10 youth for overnight. We sang Easter songs & played volleyball. Crowd @ Sam Ms.

Tuesday, April 12, 1977. Daffodils are in bloom on east side of house. I washed. Was very drying weather with a warm south wind. I also planted lettuce, radishes, kohlrabi, & 1 lb. #9 peas (5 long rows).

Wednesday, April 13, 1977. Two of our apricot trees are blooming. I ironed and removed feed bugs from raspberry plants. Felt so "all in" in P.M. Baby now notices her feet. In evening I planted 2 rows Kennebec potatoes. Sunny & cloudy. Baby slept most of day.

Thursday, April 14, 1977. It rained a nice shower. I changed diapers and fed little ones. Managed to put new & longer sleeves into my black pageant crepe dress [a trade name for the fabric] & lengthened the cape. Was tired in evening even though I didn't get a lot done.

Friday, April 15, 1977. 94 in sun. I pressed sunpants & dresses. In A.M. I rocked both girlies, showing Katie pictures from the *Bible*

Primer. She liked the "horsie" that carried Mary & Baby Jesus.

Saturday, April 16, 1977. I washed diapers before breakfast. It took so long to wash yesterday's breakfast, lunch, and supper dishes, & cream coolers. By the time they were done, it was time to start dinner! I dusted.

Sunday, April 17, 1977. We attended Sunday School. Acts 16 was our lesson. James Bontrager, Al Beiler are teachers. Went to Joseph Ys for dinner. Had fresh rhubarb pie. Ate popcorn and drank chocolate milk at home before chores.

Monday, April 18, 1977. Lettuce & radishes are up. Nice day. I washed and ironed. ESFs were here for supper. Edna & Eli mulched the Kennebecs. Fannie sat on the small folding chair & Katie couldn't stand it. (I paddled.)

Tuesday, April 19, 1977. 'Twas bake day. Bread, rolls, cookies proceeded from the oven. We had fresh rhubarb for supper & cookies. Apple trees are in bloom. Lilacs have begun, too. Daffodils are withered. Peas are peeping.

Wednesday, April 20, 1977. Foggy in morning. Now sunny & warm. Both daughters slept long in A.M. Baby nursed at dinner [picture of table] then returned to sleep again. She's so "brauf!"

Thursday, April 21, 1977. Felt very blue. Bathed my daughters & shampooed my head, washed diapers, & put trash room in order. Katie like being upstairs, too, but when she saw Daddy from [picture of window] she said, "Daddy, Doppa [hurry]!" She wanted to join him.

Friday, April 22, 1977. Eli took me up to Jonah Clara in morning & returned to work. I visited there, then went to Cottonwood Grove picnic with Willies. Eli came back for dinner & helped play ball. Katie enjoyed her first swing ride in my lap. Baby was good @ school.

Saturday, April 23, 1977. Ray came in morning. He mowed, piled tree trimmings, & helped Eli move straw & sheep. Was here overnight. I dusted, got meals, & washed dishes. After baths we crawled to bed, late again.

Sunday, April 24, 1977. We attended church at Charles Benders. Peter T. Yoder preached. We sang for Fred Fisher in P.M. He had his 8oth birthday. Were at ESFs for supper.

Monday, April 25, 1977. I washed bedding and diapers, etc. Baby was fussy in A.M., a reaction of my condition yesterday probably in part. I folded and put wash away. I opened up the last jar of vegetable soup.

Tuesday, April 26, 1977. Very warm. Fellowship School had a wiener roast in James's timber. They walked on left side of road by twos with teacher Dorothy Lapp in rear. I hoed & baked Pride of Iowa cookies. Seems my mood for working is lagging.

Wednesday, April 27, 1977. Sunny & warm wind. I planted 49 non-acid tomato plants, baby head cabbage, 3 savory plants, carrots, spinach, & big limas (pretty early for limas?). In P.M. I baked bread & rhubarb custard pies. We had some for supper.

Thursday, April 28, 1977. Baby is such a fatty. Smiles every day. Katie played doll. Has 3 all different sizes. Chilly east wind. I washed a big wash & ironed, folded & put wash away. Had roast [picture of a chicken], baked beans from scratch, corn bread, & pineapple & orange jello supper.

Friday, April 29, 1977. A heavy frost in morning. I watered garden plants b-4 breakfast, but water froze on them. Dad spent the day visiting & shelling beans, etc., here. In evening Eli & I planted baby limas & string beans (beans from my own seed—Blue Lake bush beans).

Saturday, April 30, 1977. Eli ended the job of trimming fruit trees & burned brush. I planted cukes [cucumbers] & sunflowers in same row & 2 rows of Golden Cross Bantum sweet corn, & soybeans. My peas are showing frost or ice defects!

4 Sarah the Gardener:
The Season of Growing

We garden like we sing:
We're all one voice.
Sarah Fisher

I drove the car up the gravel drive, stopped next to the bright white hitching post, and parked on the other side of Sarah's horse and buggy. The only commonality of our transportation was the color black: the Volvo sedan, the horse, the buggy. The second I stepped out of the car, I heard it. Music? On this Amish farm? I listened as I stood under the maple tree and felt the sunlight filtering through. The words were blown to me from the garden by the light breeze. I was drawn to the a capella singing:

> We have heard a joyful sound, Jesus saves, Jesus saves;
> Spread the gladness all around, Jesus saves, Jesus saves.
> Bear the news to ev'ry land,
> Climb the steps and cross the waves,
> Onward, 'tis our Lord's command, Jesus saves, Jesus saves.

I spotted the Fisher family spread across the one-acre garden, children and crops all in various growing stages. They were picking peas, pulling carrots, checking the sweet corn for ripeness, and singing.

Anna Swartz and I had come prepared to work in the garden, she in her calico sunbonnet and I in a straw hat. I felt like singing, too; if I only knew the tune. We walked over to Sarah, who was bent over picking the largest, ripest tomatoes I'd ever seen. She stood up straight, laughed and said, "Whew, it's time for a break." We moved from the humid garden and hot sun to the porch swing hanging from the maple tree. As we heard news of the last several weeks, I kept thinking about the music in the garden. How could the Fishers sound so beautiful without any accompaniment?

"You don't use any instruments, do you?" I asked.

"No, they're not allowed. Except I used to play a mouth harp for fun. Maybe with age my interests have changed, because I don't play it now. I actually learned to play it from my sister by watching her, but I played it backwards. Instead of having the high notes to the right, I held it so that they were to the left. Isn't that funny?"

"Have I told you that I play the bagpipes?" I asked. Sarah listened politely. We drank our cold water, I on the swing while Sarah rocked in the metal lawn chair. I returned to common ground. I asked, "But how do you know what note you're on? Who starts? How do you stay on pitch?"

"We don't always stay on pitch. It's sometimes a real problem at church. There is a woman who is so kind-hearted, but she does not sing with the others. You noticed it, Martha. She was there the day you and Anna were at Overholts for church. We faltered, didn't we? You heard it, didn't you?"

I felt practically Amish. She assumed I knew enough about her music to have an opinion on the singing. I had no idea.

"I really don't know," I said. "Since it was all in German and it was the first time I'd heard your church music, I was not able to tell. But how *do* you stay on pitch? How about using a pitch pipe?" I asked, thinking of my reliance on this handy tool while Christmas-caroling.

"It's not allowed," Eli said, joining us from his work on the drywalling in their new house next to the garden. "Once the first singer starts, it's up to everyone else to stay together. We don't sing parts—that's what we say—or harmony—that's what you say—at Sunday church. We're all one voice."

It sounded so poetic. To me, it also meant being of one mind, in agreement, at peace with one another. I longed to be part of a group that was all one voice. "Do you have a copy of the music you were singing? How do you know what note to start on?" I asked.

Sarah offered to lend me two books to look over at home. *Lieder-Sammlung*, exclusively words, is Eli's book, from which he sings during church services. The other, *The Church and Sunday School Hymnal*, is used during the young people's Sunday-night singings and other singings in the community. It includes both English words and music.

Eli said, "Not many of us actually read the music as notes. We don't need to. We learn it by hearing it. We listen to the first person who starts. We all follow from there." I was amazed that Sarah learns musical concepts, the relationship of notes, sound, pitch, emphasis, and expression, and the words from listening to others. I had never considered learning music any other way than with the aid of musical instruments and through the study of music theory.

Sarah told me the Amish believe that the voice is God-given and musical instruments are not. Not only are instruments not allowed; they aren't needed. I observed that while pitch matters, accuracy is judged in relation to another human being, not to a musical instrument. The voice doesn't need to be tuned like a piano or guitar; the first voice starts and the rest match it. If singing in parts, everyone else harmonizes from the starting pitch. It requires concentration and a willingness to listen to others. This is more important than singing with musical instruments or knowing which particular note is being sung.

Sarah said, "We garden like we sing: we're all one voice. Because we're all one voice, we accomplish big tasks, like taking care of this garden." The breeze picked up. We were rested and ready to work once again. To my unexpected delight, the music amidst the garden rows took up again.

Gardener at the Ready

Sarah announced we would begin by picking the Old Dark Beauties strawberries. How was I to find my way through Sarah's rows of sweet corn, beans, peas, and squash, much less the borders of Valentine rhubarb, raspberries, strawberries, and blueberries? I stood taking it all in, admiring the unending rows of petunias blooming red, white, and blue on the edge of the garden. I asked where I would find the strawberries.

Always organized, she said, "Just come down Highway 22 and duck your head as you go under the wire."

I stopped in my tracks. Highway 22? I noticed two aluminum

potatoes

black raspberry plants	Cauliflower, Eggplants, carrots	1st planting Radishes	2nd planting Potatoes
potatoes	Potatoes	1st planting Spinach	2nd planting Potatoes
black raspberry plants	Potatoes	Onions	
Sweet corn	Potatoes	Kohlrabi	
Sweet corn	Potatoes	1st planting Lettuce	2nd planting Sweet Potato
Sweet corn "Early Sunglow"	Stringbeans "Blue Lake"	Lettuce	
Sweet corn	Limabeans & Stringbeans	Cabbage & Broccoli	
Peas "Progress #9"	Peas "Early Frosty"	"Lincoln" Peas	2nd planting Potatoes
Early carrots, Pak Choi	Golden beets, Redbeets, Peanuts	Peanuts	
radishes	Potatoes, Peanuts	Peanuts	
muskmelons "star headliner"	Tomatoes	Watermelon "Charleston Gray"	
Potatoes	Potatoes	Tomatoes "Delicious"	
Potatoes	Sweet Potatoes		
Potatoes	Petunias	Petunias	

Garden Path

Garden Path

My garden is like our county. I've named the garden rows that divide it after the highways that intersect in this county.—Sarah Fisher

pie tins bent over the top strand of the woven wire fences that intersected her sizable garden.

Sarah said, "Look a little closer."

I did, and said, "This pie tin has the number one written on it and the other one has the number twenty-two. Why?"

"My garden is like our county. I've named the garden rows that divide it after the highways that intersect in this county. So I call that part of the garden the Northwest District after the church district." Her tone was humorous as she told me the meaning of the cryptic signs and pointed out how the garden mirrored the Amish church districts and specific farms within. To me, viewing the garden as the church district was an extraordinary idea. To Sarah, it solved a problem. With as many as thirty different types of fruits, vegetables, and flowers, she is able to tell one of the children which specific pea patch is ready for picking. She identifies the item as to where it correlates within the church district. The peas in question were located "at the Miller farm."

"Tell me all about your garden. How big is it? Have you grown blueberries?" Sarah asked.

My gardening efforts seemed so plain next to Sarah's. My rose garden is planted in symmetrical rows, six roses by six roses, routinely fed, watered, and dusted with bug repellent. I plant a few herbs, even tomatoes, if I'm organized enough to buy them from the local nursery in the spring. I felt wasteful and frivolous next to Sarah. My garden's purpose is to grow roses for indoor bouquets; hers is to feed a family of nine.

Sarah's bonnet shaded her face from the intense sun. She hoed the neatly ordered rows filled with peas, radishes, and lettuces.

"How did you learn about growing the raspberries, apples, and pears? How did you know how to organize this acre of garden?" I asked.

Sarah hoed and talked at the same time. "Well, I've known how for a long time. You grow up with it and learn just by watching." She patted the earth around the seeds she had just placed in the furrow. Sarah's two youngest children were at the end of the row, making dandelion chains.

"See, you have to pat them in to keep the moisture in. I learned that from my mother. One day my mother asked me to plant radish seeds, so I prepared the furrow. I decided to go inside to do some work and came back later. My mother didn't like that much. The furrows were dried out. The seeds were planted in dry soil, and they would have had some moisture if I had followed through sooner. I should have planted them and promptly covered them with the still-moist earth, then patted the earth down firmly. You need to keep the moisture in."

As we picked beautiful, robust strawberries, I asked Sarah how she foiled what I refer to as "garden enemies." She said, "Come and I'll show you the eggshells. See? I mix them into the soil. This helps keep away the slugs. They prefer moist soil and like to eat portions of the strawberry. The eggshells help keep them away."

Like the generations before them, Sarah's children learn first-hand the purposes and benefits of gardening. The children have experimented with garden keeping on a small scale. Mary grew peas and realized a profit of four dollars. Sarah's son Duane grew two rows of potatoes, sold them, and used the money to buy a new straw hat. Every year he grows gourds for use as birdhouses for the Purple Martins. Katie grows flowers for sale at the Farmers' Market.

Although I grew a peanut patch as a child, I spent more time playing Mr. McGregor and Peter Rabbit with my best friend. Sarah's children, however, are seriously involved in the daily garden-keeping activities. They are kept busy with hoeing and weeding, spraying for insects, and harvesting the ripe vegetable of the moment. As Sarah says, "There is always something that must be done in the garden. Either the insects are having their dinner, or we are. We garden every day."

Our Garden Sources

I asked Sarah how she knows so much about all the varieties of fruits and vegetables. She brought out a stack of favorite gardening books she has used since she and Eli were first married. "I read the information in the seed catalogues that I order from every year." Picking one up, Sarah laughed and read, "This tomato will blot out the sun." I said I thought that some products' names seemed to hold bigger-than-life promises: "Bodacious sweet corn" and "Miracle sweet corn." She laughed and commented, "As with any advertising, a gardener needs to be skeptical. I wonder who thinks up these names?"

Sarah and I have influenced each other in the sources we use for seeds. Thanks to Sarah, I was placed on the mailing list for Gurney's and Jung's nurseries, and when I discovered several special-interest catalogues, I shared them with Sarah. She was most intrigued with the organic gardening catalogue. I said, "The charts are helpful. At a glance you can know what soil type and growing conditions are needed."

Sarah obligingly looked at the charts and said, "I try to garden naturally, and I'll guess that the prices in this catalogue will be lower since there are black and white and no fancy color photos." We compared catalogues and prices. She was right. When I brought over the Tomato Growers Supply Company catalogue, Sarah said, "It's *all* tomatoes! I've never seen one like this. And there are peppers. Last year we had so many pests on them, a sort of a white fly. I need to learn more about peppers. They also have many varieties for early crops. I can get more produce out of the same area."

Now I garden with a purpose. Because I'm influenced by Sarah, I now have a stand of raspberries that I can pick well into fall, freezing the extra to pull out and thaw for a treat during the winter. I plan to add blueberries. Sarah's experiment worked, so it's my turn to try. I added strawberries and a snow apple tree to my garden because they came well recommended. "Strawberries are good for you. Eli's favorite apple is the snow apple because it is so white and tart, yet sweet."

Sarah's and my gardening purposes are contrasted by our choices of favorite recipes. One day she was showing me how to spray cabbage for insects, and I asked what her favorite garden recipe might be. She immediately said, "I know—the sweet dill pickle recipe. This recipe was given to me by a neighbor and is especially good for the children's school lunches." She showed me the recipe when we were back in the kitchen.

I began to read Sarah's pickle recipe aloud: "Slice cucumbers thin and—wait—what is meant by thin?"

She said, "I'll show you."

As we sliced cucumbers, I told Sarah about my favorite garden recipe, given to me by a friend, Ardis Anderson, who owns and operates an Iowa sheep farm. I said, "This salsa recipe works well with the amount of tomatoes that I raise and the amount of time that I have available. It's a quick salsa made even faster with the use of a blender. It takes such a minimum amount of time, I re-named it Quicksilver Salsa. If I have time, I use fresh jalapeño pepper instead of canned, chopped peppers."

Sarah looked at me and shook her head, "You don't even have time to chop up a pepper?"

The Diary as a Garden Record

Sarah refers back to her diary to check the current garden's progress. The importance of these records is evident to Sarah: "It's how I know when I planted what, what produced well and why, and what I will and will not plant again." She also keeps a more detailed notebook exclusively for gardening records. Sarah writes comments in parentheses about the items' use and success. She says her goal is to maximize the use of the space and growing sea-son. When the early peas are done, she removes the vines and plants another vegetable in the same space.

I told Sarah that I use her diary to know what to expect in my garden. Through her May entries, I know when my rhubarb might be ready and when I should trim my raspberry patch. "Why don't you start your own garden records?" she suggested. I did. Like Sarah, I include quotations. Hers originate in the Bible; mine, in Emerson.

June 12, 1994. "When it is dark enough you can see the stars." Emerson.

June 24, 1994. Sweet peas are blooming but are drying out. Idea: Plant in shady area. They'll get sun in early spring, and when it gets hot, they'll be cooler & protected.

June 30, 1994. Yesterday was 95. Deer are eating the tops of the roses. The new roses are doing well, very fragrant. I "pegged them" up on bamboo sticks.

I also note themes similar to Sarah's, what is successful and what is not. My diary is beginning to sound like Sarah's; it's just that the focus is different. She grows vegetables, fruit, and a few flowers; I grow flowers, fruit, and a few vegetables.

Sarah's priorities appear in her diary entries:

Wed., June 1, 1977. Eli & I picked 12 qt. of strawberries at Willie Yutzys before breakfast. Got some nice big ones. I sliced some to freeze & mashed others. We're getting some of our own, too, which helps out.

Tues., June 7, 1977. Peas today—peas yesterday. They surely do take time & add up slowly. While Eli was at work our 231 Dekalb chicks came and 1500 of them! ESF came along with the driver. For each 100 we got 2 extra.

Crops are as negotiable as crisp dollar bills in Sarah's world. Sometimes the garden output is an unexpected but desirable way to pay for services:

Wed., June 8, 1977. I finally found time to wash this week. In P.M. Dale Miller brought us a gallon of sour cherries as payment for what Eli fixed on his tractor lately. I folded & put away wash.

We finished our work late that day in the garden. Sarah was barefoot, the sleeves of her long cotton dress pushed up. Beneath my long, khaki skirt my gardening moccasins were caked with evening dew and dirt turning to mud. Handing me the garden hose, Sarah said, "Now do you see why I go barefoot? One stop at the hose, and no more mud!" Next time, I thought as I washed off my shoes. I walked to my car and loaded the tomatoes Sarah had given me into the trunk.

Standing on the back steps of Sarah's house, I stopped to look at her garden acre. From the vivid colors, I could identify the garden varieties: Wizard of Oz Emerald City green cucumbers; burgundy beets, recently pulled, and waiting to be washed; raspberries, such a deep ruby they appeared artificial. The yellow and green squashes were barely visible through leaves the size of umbrellas. Sarah's garden provided far more intense and vibrant color than any of my old-fashioned roses.

The sun was going down, and the day was cooling off. I walked toward the garden through layers of hot and cool air. Sarah appeared from the arbor carrying a bushel basket partially full of ripe grapes. In her pale lavender dress, she blended into the garden landscape. A blue jay scolded from a tree.

Sarah called, "Martha, let's sing this one:"

> The God of harvest praise;
> In loud thanksgiving raise hand, heart, and voice;
> The valleys smile and sing,
> Forests and mountains ring,
> The plains their tribute bring,
> The streams rejoice.

> The God of harvest praise;
> Hearts, hands, and voices raise,
> With sweet accord;
> From field to garner throng,
> Bearing your sheaves along,
> And in your harvest song,
> Praise ye the Lord.

SARAH'S GARDEN LIST

> Blue Lake Bush beans (produce buckets and buckets of beans)
> Old Dark Beauties strawberries (tasty)
> Miracle sweet corn
> Bodacious sweet corn
> Early Sunglow corn (very early and very successful)
> ming choy (an experiment; eat it like celery)

Usually the woman and girls in the family do the lawn mowing. I keep our mower in good repair.—Sarah Fisher

Kennebec potatoes (grown from our seed; use as an ingredient in rolls)

pear tomatoes (provide variety)

nonacid tomatoes (a nice alternative)

Puerto Rican (maple leaf) sweet potatoes

kohlrabi (red and white; good when peeled like an onion and eaten raw)

ground cherries (good for use in pies)

Charleston Gray watermelon

Dixie Queen watermelon

Hearts of Gold muskmelons

Iroquois muskmelons

Valentine rhubarb (sweet and tart at the same time)

eggplant (husband isn't fond of this)

Summertime head lettuce

Jumbo peanuts

pumpkins

cabbage

SARAH'S FAVORITE SWEET DILL RECIPE

Slice cucumbers thin and put in canning jars. Add a garlic bud and some dill on top. Heat and pour over cucumbers the following ingredients (to make a larger batch use the quantities that appear in parentheses):

2 (8) cups vinegar
2 (8) cups water
3 (12) cups sugar
2 (8) tablespoons salt

Cold pack for 5 minutes after they have come to a hard boil. This should be enough for 8 pints (4 quarts).

MARTHA'S QUICKSILVER SALSA

1 cup finely chopped, peeled tomatoes
1 four-ounce diced, canned jalapeño peppers (drained) OR
   2 small fresh jalapeño peppers, chopped
several dashes bottled hot pepper sauce
1 to 2 tablespoons snipped cilantro (optional)
1/2 cup canned tomato sauce
1/4 cup sliced green onions
2 tablespoons lemon juice
1 clove minced garlic

Combine all ingredients. Place half the mixture in a blender. Blend until smooth. Stir in the remaining mixture. Cover and chill. Serve with tortilla chips. Makes 2 cups.

May, June, July, and August 1976

Saturday, May 1, 1976. In A.M. I baked 2 rhubarb custard pies, mopped kitchen, & dusted living room, bedrooms, also spaded part of strawberry bed. In P.M. Eli tilled & I trimmed raspberry plants.

Sunday, May 2, 1976. After Sunday School we had 3 Jamesport, Missouri dinner guests. The Hershberger sisters were ex-pupils of mine.

Monday, May 3, 1976. Very windy. I washed. The diapers really fluffed up nicely. In P.M. I finished the baby quilt by putting on the binding. Eli helped me fold wash after supper.

Tuesday, May 4, 1976. Today Katie is 7 months old. She is beginning to creep. I planted ferns along north side of hen house that Eli brought home last evening from Jonah Claras. Also made a new white cap for me.

Wednesday, May 5, 1976. Katie crept to me as I squatted down a few feet from her. Daddy saw her creep for first time after supper. Dorothy Swartz made a surprise visit in A.M. I ironed & pressed Sunday pants, etc.

Thursday, May 6, 1976. Cool and cloudy in A.M. Elsie Ann Troyer became bride of Mark Miller today. They wed in the barn. Was cold. Women wore their shawls. We were there in evening, too.

Friday, May 7, 1976. I planted 29 young raspberry plants that Eli got yesterday P.M. @ Lloyd Helmeths. Also hoed in garden. Pops were here in P.M. Mom brought goods for baby, a suit, & cut it here. We tilled & planted spuds & cukes in evening.

Saturday, May 8, 1976. Sunny, not as windy as yesterday. Eli mulched grapevines & raspberry plants with corn stalk bales that we had around the house for winter insulation. I mowed.

Sunday, May 9, 1976. Preacher Jeremiah Ropp & Vernon Bender preached @ Michael Yoders. Small gma. Went to old people's singing in evening at Sam Millers.

Monday, May 10, 1976. I beat husband out to the barn in morning. There lay Blackie in misery, a filly dead & not fully born! The vet didn't come until after the second call. My, I really pitied Blackie! I washed. Sunny & warm.

Tuesday, May 11, 1976. Warm & dry. I planted Iowa & Illini Chief sweet corn, tomatoes, water & muskmelons. We had fresh radishes for supper. Isaac T. took baby & me to Kalona when he went to get the school bus. We both took treatments from Dr. Winters.

Wednesday, May 12, 1976. Early @ dawn I got up & watered raspberry plants in my nightgown! Couldn't sleep anyhow. Also planted 1 double row of peas b-4 breakfast & another afterwards, plus potatoes & red beets. I cleaned up the MESSY wash house. Got 2 dead dried-up rats!

Thursday, May 13, 1976. Beautiful rain in morning. Eli heard it rain last night (I didn't). B-4 breakfast I scattered lettuce seed in the rain! I refixed my gray dress & apron making them larger!

Friday, May 14, 1976. I got equipment ready for baby chicks. They came—100 fuzzy baby "peepers." A swing door was woman-made & hung on west side of wash house. In P.M. dandelion heads were mown off but I wasn't done when hubby came home.

Saturday, May 15, 1976. Katie raised herself up in bed alone for first time. We have 1 dead chick already. I sewed curtains & hung them in wash house. Rained in A.M. Sunny in P.M.

Sunday, May 16, 1976. Had small Sunday Schoolaf [School]. We were at Jacobs for dinner. Kenny has changed his looks. Is fatter.

Monday, May 17, 1976. Very windy from north. Big white bunches of clouds in sky. We didn't have enough heat for our chicks. 8 are dead! I fixed a crude roof over pen & added a second lantern. Eli & I demolished the corn crib in evening. (I washed today.)

Tuesday, May 18, 1976. With the aid of the wheelbarrow I dumped loads of firewood into the wash house & cleaned up in lot west of barn. In evening Isaac T. was here & helped move the brooder house to west side of barn. (I ironed in P.M.)

Wednesday, May 19, 1976. Lovely—The Mrs. hoed in A.M. & did some fixing jobs in wash house & on the outside. Katie tried to do "patty-cake" by herself. She tore a hole on the inside of her bottom lip with the end of a coat hanger used to hold up the diaper stacker that was hanging over her bed.

Thursday, May 20, 1976. Very warm—Mom, Bertha, Mae Faye, Amos Lydie, & I were at Lloyds to celebrate Ann Marie's 37th birthday. I brought home clothes for baby that were Barbara's [Ann Marie's daughter]. Transplanted head lettuce in evening that Mom gave me.

Friday, May 21, 1976. The chicks got extra care this A.M. I cleaned their pen & put in a different hover [a cover to keep chicks warm]. In P.M. I baked chocolate cake, 2 cherry pies, 4 loaves bread, made apple jello, & finished the mowing I'd begun in A.M. ESFs were here in evening for ice cream.

Saturday, May 22, 1976. [picture of dark cloud] Cloudy. Oh, that nice oriole! She's building her nest out east somewhere. I saw her tugging for all she was worth out the east kitchen window. Eli told me to hang out string. I did & in a short time she was there, got a piece & flew away with the string flying out behind! Now she's making trips for more.

Sunday, May 23, 1976. Eli has the flu so we stayed home. Our gma was @ Lloyd Bs. We missed out on our invitation to Josephs. Eli was first to discover Katie's lower incisor now through.

Monday, May 24, 1976. I got a late start washing, but Katie was very happy so I had hung up about all the wash by 12:30. I ironed in P.M. & folded & put away clothes. In evening I held the squealing pigs while Eli cut off tails, etc.

Tuesday, May 25, 1976. A sunny & very nice day. Katie was fussy. She is teething & her nose & eyes run over! (Cries.) I washed down the kitchen ceiling & walls except the east one. Eli planted cane in evening with a "contraption" that saved a lot of time. Looks sort of like a scooter.

Wednesday, May 26, 1976. Katie now holds her bottle to drink milk. I planted coleus & begonias on south side of house, fixed a pen for my chicks & put 'em in, sprayed fruit trees, & cut "Missie" a light blue suit. Nice & warm. Peonies are beginning to bloom.

Thursday, May 27, 1976. The whole family was bathed & dressed in Sun. clothes as we set out for James Bontragers. We walked & carried baby. Saw an indigo bunting & catbird along the way. Rebecca served a bounteous dinner.

Friday, May 28, 1976. Katie walks around in her bed by holding on. Today she pulled herself up by the rocker & stood rocking it. Little Betz [a term of endearment for Katie]! I hoed in the garden & planted squash, marigolds, sweet potatoes (& cabbage yet in evening with Eli's help).

Saturday, May 29, 1976. It rained a lot today. Good for us to have done transplanting yesterday. I sewed on Katie's suit from Mom, & mended clothes in P.M.

Sun., May 30, 1976. We attended Sunday School. Had dinner at Dale Millers & supper at my folks.

Monday, May 31, 1976. I washed & went to Lester Yoders & got a baby bed, wardrobe, hamper, etc., from garage sale items Mae had gotten. ESFs were here except Pop. Mom & Leah washed down bedroom. Wanda hung up wash.

Tuesday, June 1, 1976. Cloudy—I mowed and folded and put wash away. We attended a McNess Meeting [home shopping meeting for household products] at Mark Fishers in evening. I was lucky enough to win a can of hand cleaner. The agent stood by his charts & talked & little Katie was lost in observation! Little pupil!

Wednesday, June 2, 1976. Oh, I've got a mean head cold. Nice & sunny. I crawled to bed in A.M. In P.M. I shelled popcorn outdoors with my back toward the sun. I sat Katie beside me on a spread, but she crawled off heading for the family of nursing cats!

Thursday, June 3, 1976. Sunny. I left Katie @ James Bontragers & went to Kalona making calls here & there first. Visited John T. Mae. Bill Stuzman shod Blackie all around for $8.24. Was at Pops for dinner.

Friday, June 4, 1976. I moved the small chest into Katie's room & hung her dresses in the wardrobe. A quick spread & quilt were made for her for everyday. Some sewing for her, too, was done.

Saturday, June 5, 1976. I planted petunias, marigolds, & sweet alyssums on east side of house & mulched them with grass clippings. In P.M. I washed down the bathroom. Were to Mary Cobbs for ice cream in evening.

Sunday, June 6, 1976. We went to church @ Lloyd Bs. In P.M. to Peter Ts to see baby Hannah.

Monday, June 7, 1976. I hurried me (ha). In A.M. in less than 3 hours time I had washed down most of the living room. At noon I milked Marigold. Eli fed the pigs & we set off until the evening. Were at crowd at Charles Bs & at Mark Fs for supper.

Tuesday, June 8, 1976. Such a huge wash. There were between 250–300 pieces with plastics [baby's plastic pants] included. I washed our buggy and folded & put away clothes. Dry & warm. Had first head lettuce.

Wednesday, June 9, 1976. I left the breakfast dishes unwashed and began hoeing. Such hard ground! I mowed and in P.M. ironed. We had roast beef, potato salad, apple jello, & pumpkin bars for supper.

Thursday, June 10, 1976. Rained in morning. I read and answered the family circle letter & patched hubby's socks.

Friday, June 11, 1976. I picked 5 gallons of peas & froze about all of them. In evening Eli helped ESF put up hay. I hoed sweet corn by moonlight. Sat on porch & waited, but he didn't come, so went to bed.

Saturday, June 12, 1976. Eli tilled in the garden for me & I hoed. It was warm but breezy & windy in P.M. I picked a couple strawberries & made a strawberry dessert. Baby & I each were bathed before supper.

Sunday, June 13, 1976. We attended Sunday school. Attendance: 148. Had dinner at Al Beilers & supper at David Overholts. Drove home in rain. There was lightning, too.

Monday, June 14, 1976. It rained & the sun shone. In between showers I hung out wash. Folded diapers, scrubbed siding of wash house porch, (now that's done once!) & in evening Eli & I picked peas. They yielded about 8 pints.

Tuesday, June 15, 1976. Cool & cloudy in morning. I got to bed @ 10:30 last evening & I feel it. Garden is very wet. Before breakfast I changed Katie's clothes. She was grouchy so I put her back to bed & she fell asleep again.

Wednesday, June 16, 1976. I weighed 150 lbs. before breakfast. Katie pulled herself up by the gas stove & enjoyed looking at my reflection as I was washing woodwork. She'd look at my reflection, then turn her head & look at me. I washed down wash room, picked peas, & baked bread, pie, & rolls.

Thursday, June 17, 1976. Katie was in bed until about 10:00 A.M., much longer than usual. In A.M. I sprayed fruit trees & stemmed strawberries we picked last evening at Willie Yutzys. I mowed in P.M. & trimmed along the walk.

Friday, June 18, 1976. Katie had a fast stroller ride down hill toward James Bontragers on the road with Mother running & guiding stroller. I helped Rebecca get ready for gma. Lloyds & Foes were here in evening with ice cream.

Saturday, June 19, 1976. Eli & I picked 30 qt. of strawberries at Ed

Yoders & Willie Hochstetlers. I canned 21 qt. & put some to freeze. We picked peas in evening. Both were tired. Got to bed late.

Sunday, June 20, 1976. Church at James Bontragers. Wanda and Dan were here for supper. We went to the singing at Jameses.

Monday, June 21, 1976. Warm—not much breeze. I washed & ironed. Katie isn't safe on the stroller anymore. Twice I found her standing up on the seat! We have 2 lame chicks out in our yard.

Tuesday, June 22, 1976. Last night a thief came & stole the bigger lame chick. Maybe it was a raccoon. I grabbed the flashlight but nothing could I see nor hear of it anymore in the dark. I pulled weeds in the cane patch.

Wednesday, June 23, 1976. Eli sold pigs at the Sale Barn. I washed windows indoors & out, and washed off other things in the kitchen.

Thursday, June 24, 1976. Our faithful "Beautiful Gal" [the horse] hauled Katie & me to Lloyds. I picked strawberries & brought home a bunch. Eli tilled in the garden for me.

Friday, June 25, 1976. The garden was hoed by me such as it will be for the time being. I picked beans (so full they hung) & canned 7 qt. Two cakes, pudding, & carrot salad were made. Then there were so-o many dishes to wash.

Saturday, June 26, 1976. Eli picked over 1 qt. of raspberries. We went to the last Jonah Fishers' descendants reunion at Wallace Fishers. In evening Eli mowed & I got ready for company tomorrow.

Sunday, June 27, 1976. Sunday School attendance: 145. We had ESFs, FBMs, Isaac & Rosemary, Charles Benders, Emmanuel Ina, Clara, & girls here for dinner.

Monday, June 28, 1976. A strong wind blew down our apricot tree on west side of hen house last night. Our little miss is understanding conversation. She understands "Kitty." Yesterday I told her a few times to make patty-cake & she did! I washed.

Tuesday, June 29, 1976. After breakfast dishes were washed & Katie still in bed I went back to bed & slept! Well, with all the efforts to get ready for Sunday's guests & Isaac Troyers here for a waffle supper last evening, I needed rest.

Wednesday, June 30, 1976. Peters left after breakfast for home with their driver. They & Emery Troyers had been on a western trip. I canned peas & beans. Katie had a lot of fun crawling after the kittens. ESFs were here in evening.

Thursday, July 1, 1976. I bathed Katie & before I got her dressed old Marigold stepped out of the water tank & went up to Isaac Ts. When we got her back baby was standing in her bed & crying. (I was so provoked over our cow!)

Friday, July 2, 1976. I made Katie a Sunday cap, pulled weeds in the cane patch, folded & put away wash & fixed trousers. In evening we went to ESFs for supper. Eli helped tear down the old [picture of a house].

Saturday, July 3, 1976. No hoeing in garden or mowing all week. We overslept & were late all day. Our small brown refrigerator was exchanged for a giant white one today. I did a job necessary 3 months ago—clean gas range.

Sunday, July 4, 1976. Many Indiana strangers in gma at James Bontragers. They had a married folks' singing in evening.

Monday, July 5, 1976. I washed a big, big, wash. Had towels & diapers washed b-4 breakfast. On dinner table we had fresh from the garden beans, kohlrabi, onion, cucumbers (slaw). Sunny & dry & warm.

Tuesday, July 6, 1976. I picked beans & cucumbers, & pulled out late pea plants & plucked & put to freeze 5 boxes. It rained a little shower after we were in bed.

Wednesday, July 7, 1976. I hoed in garden in A.M. Katie was so happy today. She occupied herself in bed most of A.M. sleeping &

playing. I canned 3 qt. cucumbers & sprayed fruit trees. ESFs brought peaches in evening.

Thursday, July 8, 1976. I'm washing dishes for first time today @ 6:30 P.M. I hoed, baked bread & cookies, & sewed. Katie is south of house in playpen. She was so quiet so I went to investigate. There she sat in contentment, playing with a teacup that was mine years ago (a favorite toy of hers).

Friday, July 9, 1976. Wanda & Leah were here & helped me dress 26 fryers. I ironed yet outdoors after sun was down.

Saturday, July 10, 1976. Our Little Sunshine Girl now holds up her patty to make "hi." She was such a good girl this A.M. I canned 11 qt. peaches & put 4 qt. raw in "frig." In evening I canned 8 qt. cucumbers & gave Eli a haircut.

Sunday, July 11, 1976. Were in Sunday School, then home for dinner. Was very warm.

Monday, July 12, 1976. Eli scratched off paint on north side of barn. I washed, ironed, & mended, & picked a lot of pickles. Sunny & nice. Katie slept long in P.M.

Tuesday, July 13, 1976. I canned pickles b-4 anyone came to help get ready for church. We canned beans, cleaned in cellar, made noodles & undercoated barn. Sunny & warm.

Wednesday, July 14, 1976. Eli pulled out the rods of the deep well by hand & had me to help him. Ann Marie brought Mae Annie & Susan to help. We cleaned upstairs, porch, living room, & worktable drawers.

Thursday, July 15, 1976. Cloudy & rainy morning. I started the task of cleaning the wash house. Mom baked cookies, Bertha cleaned 2 downstairs bedrooms, & James Rebecca washed chairs & cupboard dishes, etc.

Friday, July 16, 1976. I baked 3 batches of bread & 1 batch of rolls. Mark Erma cleaned bathroom & passage way. Dale Wanda cleaned front entrance & Lettie Faye cleaned in kitchen. Was well ready by evening.

Saturday, July 17, 1976. I hoed in garden & made another batch of rolls & 8 pies. In P.M. I helped fix & erect tent for church. In evening we mowed & burned trash. Got to bed late.

Sunday, July 18, 1976. Church was well attended. Both our folks were here. Katie was feverish & sick. All the 8 pies were devoured.

Monday, July 19, 1976. I tidied up house, washed breakfast dishes & laid down to rest before I began with the washing. Naturally it was late when I got done. In evening I canned 4 qt. of sweet corn.

Tuesday, July 20, 1976. I hung up the remainder of the clothes and canned 5 qt. of sweet corn & recanned 4 qt. of red beets left over from Sunday. It really rained in evening. Was hard on the tent.

Wednesday, July 21, 1976. The relief sewing was here. Was cloudy most of the day. We quilted under the tent in P.M. Attendance in all was over 50 (large).

Thursday, July 22, 1976. Mom stayed for sewing & was here last night. Eli beheaded the first 12 fryers before he left for work. In all, Mom & I dressed 25. A woman from Lima, Illinois, got 24. I took Mom to town.

Friday, July 23, 1976. Quite a week—sewing—fryers—now going away. I had dinner at Lettie Fishers, then bought grocery shower gifts in town & went out to Mark Millers for the occasion. Warm. Blackie sweated.

Saturday, July 24, 1976. Now it's get ready for company, but there are cucumbers to can, apricots & apples to gather, & corn to process. Eli washed dishes twice today & brought in the apricots. I canned 21 qt. pickles, baked buns, 2 cakes, & 6 apple pies.

Sunday, July 25, 1976. Another warm day. We attended Sunday School, then went to Lloyds for dinner. We had 18 folks including married couples here for supper & singing afterwards.

Monday, July 26, 1976. [picture of umbrella and rain] I washed a big wash. My two lines are never enough to hold all the diapers, shirts, etc. Dale Miller & Lettie were here in P.M. They got cucumbers & apples. Katie now makes good-bye.

Tuesday, July 27, 1976. I felt lazy. Did the ironing & patched clothes.

Wednesday, July 28, 1976. Our Little Miss is quite a gal. Today she grabbed one of my footlets & tore off with it on purpose, but Mama got it back. I made 1 gallon of apricot jam. Probably won't take all of it though for church. It surely can rain & rain. Rained twice today.

Thursday, July 29, 1976. The housewife turned out 18 loaves of bread, 4 mince pies, & canned 7 qt. of Melba [a variety of apple] applesauce besides keeping about 3 qt. to eat.

Friday, July 30, 1976. Vera & children, Edna & girls were here. We had a good dinner of frier meat, dressing, ice cream, & warm apple pie, etc. I made 12 more loaves of bread & 4 pumpkin pies. Other work was butchering fryers, canning 16 qt. pickles, freezing 10 qt. sweet corn, and baking cookies.

Saturday, July 31, 1976. Vera was here & did good work in cleaning for tomorrow. I baked 2 pans of rolls & washed diapers, set 2 tables in basement, etc. Eli mowed & pulled weeds for me.

Sunday, August 1, 1976. Beautiful morning. Church was here under the tent. ESFs & FBMs were here & all my brothers & sisters except Lloyds. Much bread left over.

Monday, August 2, 1976. I held Katie, showing her pictures from *Good Morning Farm.* She recognized the kittens & liked that picture.

Tuesday, August 3, 1976. I recanned leftover preserves and red beets & pickles from Sunday. Dale Vera & Lettie were here to pick cucumbers. I picked our first ripe tomatoes, big onions, & dug potatoes. In P.M. I ironed.

Wednesday, August 4, 1976. What a lot of time I spent on a little doll's dress. Bertha gave a tiny wooden doll for Katie so I'm fixing her up for Sunday play. I made a blue dress for Katie. The goods was given by Dan Kathryn.

Thursday, August 5, 1976. Katie & Mama went to Kalona to Pops. My other married sisters came, too, to help get ready for church. In P.M. we went up to David Fishers, where church is to be & cleaned etc. there. Our chicks came today—100 meat makers.

Friday, August 6, 1976. The cool weather in A.M. inspired me to make vegetable soup. I canned 14 qt., also canned 8 pt. of sweet corn. Had so many dishes to do. Then in evening I washed off buggy. Was moonlight when I pulled it away. Eli left in evening for Cedar Rapids.

Saturday, August 7, 1976. My night last night was a bad one. My sinuses were blocked. I finally fell asleep on sofa maybe around 3:00. Eli went to help his folks with the new shop. Baby was fussy. Maybe she missed her Daddy, as she didn't see him this morning & only a little last evening.

Sunday, August 8, 1976. My folks served eats today @ church @ David Fs in town so we went. All of our family from Iowa was there. Lloyd Helmuth & Yoder preached.

Monday, August 9, 1976. I washed but didn't iron. In P.M. I cut some clothes for Katie. Larry Benders were here in evening to see if Eli would do their chores during their Missouri trip. Nice big moon in evening.

Tuesday, August 10, 1976. I left my ironing be and sat down to sew. The Mrs. Sew and Sew brought forth a yellow gown for Katie & an aqua gown. The materials were given by Andy Vera & Joni Grace, respectively.

Wednesday, August 11, 1976. Last evening we went to ESFs. Eli wanted to work on the new shop's garage door, but instead we went to Sam Millers & ate ice cream. Jonah Bylers of Canada were there. I sewed.

Thursday, August 12, 1976. Eli went to work again as usual & as usual I packed his lunch. In A.M. I went to Lawrence Rebecca's store & bought some materials, thread, & buttons. Also, a toy watch for Katie & a beaded little coin purse.

Friday, August 13, 1976. Irma & Frieda Bontrager were here because Rebecca had gone to help get ready for church at David Overholts. I finished Katie's suit (green) from my material leftover. We went to ESFs in evening. Eli helped with garage door.

Saturday, August 14, 1976. Eli took sick last night. Today he is in bed. I did his chores & mine, canned tomato juice, and mowed lawn.

Sunday, August 15, 1976. Eli did not feel well enough to go to church so we stayed home. Such a lovely day.

Monday, August 16, 1976. There was no white shirt nor organdy Sunday apron in the wash today [Eli's Sunday shirt and Sarah's Sunday apron]. Nevertheless my wash was big enough anyhow. In P.M. I ironed. In evening we visited John Miller in the hospital and then went fishing. Eli caught a 23″ [picture of fish]. I didn't fish.

Tuesday, August 17, 1976. I canned tomato juice and 2 qt. applesauce. These are pink now because of the red skins. I also cut 3 slips for Katie unless I decide to give one away.

Wednesday, August 18, 1976. Katie & I went to a Lone Star quilting at Fred & Leah's place. I was to bring a guest so mine was Bill F. Susan. We had good mashed potatoes, chicken, etc. In evening I began sewing small slips.

Thursday, August 19, 1976. Katie & I went to church services at David Fs for visiting ministers of Indiana. We went with James Bontragers. I washed my breakfast dishes in P.M. & sewed.

Friday, August 20, 1976. I held Katie as Eli rode off to work. For the first time she cried when seeing Daddy go away. I finished sewing the 3 little slips & made myself a Sunday half slip of white. I made cake & carrot salad for tomorrow & boiled eggs.

Saturday, August 21, 1976. Sunny & warm. Eli took a bushel of Melba apples to Wilsons, then rode on to Bill Masts to help put up ESFs tent for the John reunion. He returned, got ready, & attended. Attendance: 579.

Sunday, August 22, 1976. Sunday School attendance: 151. Lessons: Acts 5−6. An Iowa City professor was there. We were home for dinner. Had chicken & noodles, chocolate cake, & peaches.

Monday, August 23, 1976. I washed & had most of it up on the lines by 11:00. In P.M. I ironed as "Missie" slept. Good ironing time then. She can't meddle around the ironing board that way. We picked pretty peaches in evening. Will have some to work up tomorrow.

Tuesday, August 24, 1976. That little Katie managed to get the heavy *Organic Gardening & Farming Encyclopedia* out of the bookshelf & is playing with it. This A.M. in her bed she watched her mouth in a small mirror I gave her to play with as she tried to make bubbles.

Wednesday, August 25, 1976. I fixed about 1 gallon of coleslaw & took it to Joes for dinner. Then we forgot to set it on the table. The dinner was to be on behalf of Johns, but they didn't show up! So we still had a Fisher get together! I got prune plums at Lloyds.

Thursday, August 26, 1976. I discovered Katie's new tooth—her upper left lateral incisor. Maybe it was there already Monday or Tuesday. She likes to play with the sewing matching belt. I canned 12 qt. plums & 10 qt. peaches & 8 qt. tomato juice.

Friday, August 27, 1976. So far I haven't sewed 1 stitch for our trip the whole week! I got Blackie shod at Stuzmans, shopped, & visited Rebecca Miller. In evening after supper, Katie took 2 steps all by herself!

I need to can about 200 quarts of vegetables each summer to feed my family and visitors each year. That's 200 quarts of corn, 200 quarts of beans, 200 quarts of peas . . . —Sarah Fisher

Saturday, August 28, 1976. A beautiful day. Lovely blue sky. A busy day, too. I canned & froze about 15 qt. peaches, baked bread & rolls, & did Saturday cleaning. Eli helped Amos by beginning installment of diesel engine.

Sunday, August 29, 1976. Baptismal services @ David Overholts for Charles Miller, Glen Yoder, Amos Miller. We hadn't known it so I had on gray dress instead of black. Via home we visited 87 year old Ann B. Were @ Jacobs in evening for birthday social for Susan.

Monday, August 30, 1976. Katie's right upper lateral incisor is through now. Last evening at Jacobs she was feverish & didn't feel well. Today she was so content I couldn't believe it. I washed. A beautiful day. (Baby was not content all along though.)

Tuesday, August 31, 1976. Last evening Erma brought peach plums. I canned 18 qt. & put stones in ground on north side of barn. Also canned 2 qt. peaches & 7 qt. tomato juice & sewed a suit together for Katie.

May, June, July, and August 1977

Sunday, May 1, 1977. Bless the Lord oh, my soul. Let the glad tidings roll. It is the holy Sabbath. To Sunday School we go. We cannot appreciate it enough. Acts 17 & 18 our Lesson. Had dinner at Emmanuel John Yoders. Were at home in evening.

Monday, May 2, 1977. I planted 2 more rows of Golden Cross Bantum sweet corn, 1 row of black raspberries, cabbage, & pepper seeds. In P.M. I bought a brown 6 year old crib from Lester Mae for $25, 3 fitted crib sheets, & an adding machine for Eli. In evening I planted winter onions from Rosemary.

Tuesday, May 3, 1977. Cloudy all day—some rain. I washed. Ann Mary folded towels & diapers. Barbara gave Katie stroller rides which she liked. I ironed in evening & made "smear case" [also known as smear cheese]. Eli helped James in cleaning up the timber in evening.

Wednesday, May 4, 1977. We went to Fellowship School's end of the year picnic. Katie loved the swing rides. Daddy hit 3 home-runs. Baby Barbara slept inside amidst the noise of the pupils in A.M. Cloudy, rainy—Earls came for more eggs & brought mush-rooms. I rearranged the nursery, 2 beds now. Baby was happy in her crib. Katie slept in the brown one.

Thursday, May 5, 1977. Barbara likes her change of bed. She slept well. I fixed lunches before I nursed her in morning. Sunny morn-ing & freshly washed. The "smear case" is good, not too stiff & not too thin! Katie said, "Potty" so I put her on.

Friday, May 6, 1977. Cloudy. Baby had bath. I set her on infant seat. She was so "talkative" to Mother—cooed. She follows me with her pretty blue eyes. I planted everbearing strawberries— climbers, sweet potatoes, geraniums, melons, & glads. I got wet from rain.

Saturday, May 7, 1977. Beautiful morning—sunny, but wet & chilly. Eli feels better after coming home sick last evening. I did cleaning. I plucked a fern peony and put it in the rose bowl. Looked pretty.

Sunday, May 8, 1977. We attended church at Charles Benders. In P.M. we visited at Fred Schwartz & Nathan I. Yoder. A Swiss couple were @ Yoders. ESFs were here for supper.

Monday, May 9, 1977. Had a late start in washing. Folded some wash, made soda cheese [a type of homemade cheese], & macaroni salad. Went to ESFs for supper in honor of Edna as yesterday was Mother's Day. All children were there.

Tuesday, May 10, 1977. Had a tough start getting off to the sewing at Charles Benders. Then I didn't get much done. In evening we planted tomato ketchup plants, eggplants, peppers, and other tomato plants in patch.

Wednesday, May 11, 1977. I put in a pretty good lick today. Went over most of the garden, spaded on west side of hen house &

cleaned fern patch. Baby coos, laughs, & kicks off stockings & booties now.

Thursday, May 12, 1977. I sewed and mowed and the baby by-yoed! (ha). I answered the family circle letter. Katie was at first afraid of the mower but became more bold & ran along beside.

Friday, May 13, 1977. My oven baked 7 loaves of bread & a chocolate cake. The wash machine washed dresses and many diapers. In evening neighbors had a wiener roast in Jameses' timber.

Saturday, May 14, 1977. I added buttonholes & buttons to Barbara's blue suit and made her a new cap. Cleaned in evening. Warm and sunny, some breeze. BCMs have first son.

Sunday, May 15, 1977. Lois helped care for our girls in Sunday School. Eli was substitute teacher for James Bontrager. We had a picnic in the Yoder timber—JDFs, JSFs, RJYs, and Lois, Paul Ys, Jerry Ys, Rachel, & Rebecca, & us, minus Katie who slept in [picture of bed]. Was fed later.

Monday, May 16, 1977. South wind—thunder—but no rain. I washed a large laundry, ironed, folded some wash & put it away. Also planted squash, hoed, & sprinkled fish oil [a fertilizer] on peas & strawberries. Peas are beginning to bloom.

Tuesday, May 17, 1977. Am tired after a big day's work yesterday. Nice morning. Partly cloudy. Grass is cold to bare feet. 3 of us had shampoos in A.M. Katie then slept so well after it. I finished braiding a swing & put it up under south maple [picture of tree] for Katie.

Wednesday, May 18, 1977. Very warm in early A.M. I felt lazy again. Got to bed late again last evening. Eli worked on tractor part for Amos T. & came home about 9:30 P.M.! So I made supper yet for him. Had daughters bathed & myself, too.

Thursday, May 19, 1977. Ascension Day. Warm & sunny. Katie enjoyed swinging in A.M. Daddy pushed her. We went to Joseph Millers in P.M. to see baby Leah. Had supper @ Pops.

Friday, May 20, 1977. I washed diapers and mowed. It started to rain in P.M. before I was done mowing so I went inside & slept. When I awoke the sun was shining beautifully. Eli came home late.

Saturday, May 21, 1977. Before breakfast I finished mowing the patch of grass I didn't get done yesterday P.M. Eli went to Kalona & other places. In P.M. Jamesport visitors called.

Sunday, May 22, 1977. We attended church at Joseph Millers. The Jamesport youth were there, too, that had stopped by yesterday. Baby acted as if she knew she were at home after gma. Lloyds came in evening.

Monday, May 23, 1977. Katie & I saw a nuthatch on the trunk on our south maple tree looking for grub. I hoed some & cleaned alongside walk that goes to barn. Baked bread and cookies. I got to bed late. Eli was there first.

Tuesday, May 24, 1977. I washed and worked outdoors. Barbara and Katie both were outdoors in P.M. I put baby in the playpen and she seemed to enjoy the outside surroundings.

Wednesday, May 25, 1977. The "cat" [bulldozer] began "dozing" [removing trees] in Jameses' stretch of timber. Today Katie hung on to my skirt pretending to swing and drive horsie (ha). I'm working outside these days. Hoed in garden.

Thursday, May 26, 1977. Today 2 cats are at work east of house. The one really creates havoc, pushing down trees and pulling out stumps. Baby was fussing today, then Katie said, "Baby." I worked outdoors again.

Friday, May 27, 1977. The whole family was bathed & dressed in Sunday clothes as we set out for James Bontragers. We walked & carried baby. Saw an indigo bunting & catbird along the way. Rebecca served us a bounteous dinner.

Saturday, May 28, 1977. More company tomorrow so that means prepare. I cooked pudding and fixed apple salad. In morning I sprinkled fish oil on raspberry & garden plants. Did Saturday cleaning. Bathed babes & myself before supper.

Sunday, May 29, 1977. Lloyds, JDFs, & JBMJrs, & Bertha were our dinner guests. We left for a very worthwhile meeting @ Sunday School house in P.M. on child training, etc. Daddy & SM did dishes. Barbara played with Katie & Bertha took care of baby.

Monday, May 30, 1977. Memorial Day, also Pentecost Monday. Youth crowd at Paul Yoders. Jonas Yoder reunion at Emmanuel Johns for which we went. Heard interesting accounts from grand-children in program.

Tuesday, May 31, 1977. As usual Eli left for work taking 2 lunches since I also fix lunch for Delmar Beiler since last fall. He pays $1.50 per lunch. I washed and put away dresses & shirts without ironing them. Saves time & gas.

Wednesday, June 1, 1977. Eli & I picked 12 qt. of strawberries at Willie Yutzys before breakfast. Got some nice big ones. I sliced some to freeze & mashed others. We're getting some of our own, too, which helps out.

Thursday, June 2, 1977. It must be that the mulberries are ripe be-cause while Katie was lying under the south maple she received a lavender wet "blotch" on her forehead! I was sitting there podding peas. ESF discovered bats in basement!

Friday, June 3, 1977. I baked bread & grapenuts & made cottage cheese curds, and washed diapers. Sunny. A squirrel was resting on a limb of the south maple tree. I almost touched its tail. It dashed up the [picture of tree].

Saturday, June 4, 1977. We picked strawberries at Willie Yutzys in morning. When it looked like rain Eli left me to get in the re-mainder of hay bales. We put them up after breakfast by our own power. Sort of fun. I canned strawberries.

Sunday, June 5, 1977. My what a humid day! Church was at Paul Yoders in hog house. David Hershberger of Ohio preached. Eli went to cellar to cool off. Ice cream would have tasted so good, but we had none!

Monday, June 6, 1977. What a contrast in weather from yesterday. Chill northern wind a-blowing. Barbara sat on high chair for first time with pillows stuffed in @ both sides. I picked and put to freeze peas. Slept in P.M. ESFs helped ready for chicks in evening.

Tuesday, June 7, 1977. Peas today—peas yesterday. They surely do take time & add up slowly. While Eli was at work our 231 Dekalb chicks came and 1500 of them! ESF came along with the driver. For each 100 we got 2 extra.

Wednesday, June 8, 1977. I finally found time to wash this week. In P.M. Dale Miller brought us a gallon of sour cherries as payment for what Eli fixed on his tractor lately. I folded & put away wash.

Thursday, June 9, 1977. I picked strawberries. Bertha & Lois came & helped me. They stemmed strawberries, seeded cherries, ironed, & picked peas from vines. I bathed baby and engineered. In evening I planted late potatoes.

Friday, June 10, 1977. Because the supper dishes weren't washed last evening, I had those to do and also finished picking peas from vines that weren't done yesterday. In evening we went to Marks. ESFs & Dans were there, too.

Saturday, June 11, 1977. Work, work—Eli fixed the weed mower and mowed weeds with it. He used the White [trade name for mower] to mow yard & the clippings to mulch potatoes. I baked bread and cherry pies, cooked pudding, etc. Also cleaned.

Sunday, June 12, 1977. Cool breeze from the east. We attended Sunday School. Our dinner guests were 3 families: Henry Fishers, Charles Beilers, David Overholts. The boys played horse with twine & looked at books. Adults visited.

Monday, June 13, 1977. Barbara is 4 months old today & weighs 17 lbs. or close by. I picked raspberries (red & black). A bug bit Eli on the tongue while eating "brockle" [milk, fruit, and cereal mixed together] soup! I pulled out strawberry plants from patch north of grapes.

Tuesday, June 14, 1977. We had our first taste of kohlrabies. I washed all of the diapers we have, & was in need of one for Katie, so pinned a pair of pink bloomers on her from the rag drawer!! Sunny and dry.

Wednesday, June 15, 1977. I milked Marigold in evening. Daddy didn't come home until bedtime. He was at Marks fixing his M.F. [Massey Ferguson tractor]. So we were late again.

Thursday, June 16, 1977. Lois had a quilting today. Participating were Ann Marie, Bertha, Susan, Mae Annie, Emmanuel Hattie, & me. We had roast beef garnished with small onions, etc. We had homemade ice cream in evening with red raspberries.

Friday, June 17, 1977. I shampooed my oily hair, then drove to Dale Millers with my girlies to help prepare for church. It rained in evening before I came home. Nice rain: 4/10″. I planted 100 Giant Robinson strawberry plants after rain in north part of garden.

Saturday, June 18, 1977. It was so cute how Katie & Barbara responded to each other this A.M., both sitting on high chairs. Katie talked to Barbara & Barbara laughed. I started a row of strawberries along south end of garden. My mom had given the plants.

Sunday, June 19, 1977. We attended church at Dale Millers & left for dinner at Mark Fs. They had much company. Baby Marvin is so small! I sat Barbara in jumper for first time. She liked it. We went to bed at daylight.

Monday, June 20, 1977. I answered my circle letter & sent a greeting to Homer Yoders and washed a big wash. In evening I baked custard & a pie shell. Eli sold 13 doz. eggs today at work for $0.40 a doz. Children were fussy in P.M.

Tuesday, June 21, 1977. I hoed in garden, transplanted purple cabbage & peppers, & ironed in A.M. The girls slept most of A.M., so different. Katie didn't call me until about 12:00. Is cloudy after dinner. I caught up diary in P.M. Was way behind!

Wednesday, June 22, 1977. Katie was very fussy. By evening my nerves were very taxed. But being able to talk with husband helped relax me. I managed to get some socks patched & began piecing a comforter for the sewing. Barbara drank 7 oz. milk.

Thursday, June 23, 1977. Cloudy. I made a Sunday blue-green dress for Katie. Had dinner at EFMs. They brought Dad home. Bontragers were there, too. In P.M. we visited. Had a nice rain in evening. Eli looked for night crawlers at bedtime.

Friday, June 24, 1977. Sultry. So very "brauf" baby Barbara. I washed diapers & baked bread. First found beans in garden! Fed Barbara beans at dinner table. She liked them. Afterwards I played with her & made her laugh out loud! Katie is better tempered today.

Saturday, June 25, 1977. In morning I cooked apricots, raspberries, Transparent apples, & spuds. We went to Susan Bontrager & Billy Byler's wedding @ Shady View Church in A.M. Reception in Kalona Recreation Center. Visited with Bertha in P.M.

Sunday, June 26, 1977. We attended church at Michael T. Yoders. Text Acts 5−6. Sermon by Andy B. Yoder. Nice day. Barbara was fussy. Mrs. Eli finally got her to sleep. Katie wore a new royal blue dress. Material from Alice Hoschstetler. MABs were here in evening.

Monday, June 27, 1977. 108 in sun in P.M. Dry grass. Melon leaves withered & very warm! I cut 3 dresses from 2 dresses & 1 apron of mine for Katie. In evening we gathered mulberries.

Tuesday, June 28, 1977. What a sudden change in weather. Cloudy & a cool wind in evening. I washed & ironed. Baby had earache in evening. I got it from her. James Rebecca cultivated in their field east of us. Katie can now crawl into her bed minus chair.

Wednesday, June 29, 1977. I finished ironing & mended clothes, canned 7 qt. mulberries & rhubarb, picked raspberries, beans, & gathered Transparent apples. In evening FFBs brought cherries (5 gallons) from Jeremiah Bontragers @ $1.50 a gallon. I seeded over half of 'em.

Thursday, June 30, 1977. Thunderstorms & rain @ 4:00 A.M. (DST). At about 4:15 I was up seeding cherries in nightgown! Eli joined me. Had 7 qt. canned b-4 breakfast. Barbara rolled over again & I didn't see her. Canned 29 qt. cherries by stretching them! Cooked apricots & canned 2 qt. Cut & sewed an everyday dress for baby from remains of my dress.

Friday, July 1, 1977. Nice day. In P.M. I sat on south side of house slicing Transparent apples—windfalls & poor quality. Eli came home from work & thought I wasted too much.

Saturday, July 2, 1977. Eli went to Kalona Park in morning to help erect tent for a family reunion. We canned 23 qt. applesauce in outdoor tank. Eli made a substitute kettle & jacket from a 50 gallon tank. It works!

Sunday, July 3, 1977. We attended church at Andy Js. Ned Yoder preached sermon. We heard him for first time. Baby did well. Charles Yoders have a Mary Ellen [baby daughter named Mary Ellen] of late. Had ice cream & pie & cold bologna in evening.

Tuesday, July 4, 1977. Eli had off. He helped me hang wash out, etc. Baby was fussy. Very warm. I folded wash & hoed strawberry patch in evening & scrubbed fruit room.

Monday, July 5, 1977. Baby slept well in A.M. Was fussy in P.M. Acts as if she were teething. I hoed flower beds & made applesauce. Have 23 qt. ready to go tomorrow morning. Cooked apples outdoors on a simple stove!

Wednesday, July 6, 1977. Eli built fire under outdoor kettle & removed 23 qt. applesauce from it (canned) after breakfast. Breeze in A.M. Baby was better today.

Thursday, July 7, 1977. Have a lot of apples to work up and am all by myself in basement slicing away. I put salt in the water & left the apple slices set overnight in the rinse tubs.

Friday, July 8, 1977. Canning applesauce today. I cooked them in the granite canner in our kettle set-up outdoors. Sauce turned out rather greenish, maybe because I had them set in tubs overnight.

Saturday, July 9, 1977. Eli helped me cut up & can applesauce. Now wasn't that nice of him. He let the first batch of apples cook too long. They got very brown. We both learned.

Sunday, July 10, 1977. Surely cooled off during night. 64 in kitchen. I wore my shawl to Sunday School & put booties & socks on Barbara. Were at home for dinner. Dad and Bertha came for overnight.

Monday, July 11, 1977. Bertha hung up wash & mowed. Place looks much better now. Dad ran errands & hoed. I washed, folded wash & got meals. In evening I cleaned refrigerator.

Tuesday, July 12, 1977. I baked a cherry pie, made ginger bars, bread, & washed dishes. Also mopped our dirty kitchen floor that I didn't do on Saturday. Cleaned wash machine.

Wednesday, July 13, 1977. Just came in from garden. And if those coons haven't visited the sweet corn patch already! Thieves! ESFs came in evening with ice cream to freeze so we ate supper outdoors. Made everyday dress for Katie.

Thursday, July 14, 1977. I finished the handwork on Katie's dress & ironed our 3 dresses b-4 breakfast that we'll wear today. Went to Elmers. Bertha took me. We patched for Mae Annie.

Friday, July 15, 1977. Rained in P.M. Mae Annie & Susan came. We worked up almost 31 qt. of apricots. Would have got more if I'd have attended to them. This way a coon stole many!! Must have climbed the [picture of a tree].

Saturday, July 16, 1977. Work, work, & fussy baby. Canned 14 qt. of sweet corn & 14 qt. more with husband's help. Got to bed way late after baths. Humid in P.M. when sun shone.

Sunday, July 17, 1977. Amos Fishers had church. We went. David & Glen B. preached. Cloudy in morning. In evening we went to Sam Millers for a family get-together. Visited, sang, & had popcorn.

Monday, July 18, 1977. Rain in A.M. I washed a huge wash. In P.M. baby cried outdoors in stroller while I was hanging up wash. I took her in my arms & started for the house & almost ran into a 27″ long snake!

Tuesday, July 19, 1977. I folded & ironed clothes. Finally got west basement scrubbed! Had wanted to for so long. Very warm. Baby plays with her feet now at 5 months old. I cleaned eggs in evening.

Wednesday, July 20, 1977. My I can't keep up with diary & work. Weeds in strawberry patch & garden, corn to process, sewing to do, but off to Kalona I go this P.M.!

Thursday, July 21, 1977. So tired from lugging my girlies around yesterday in Kalona. Katie walked beside me on walks helping to push cart, too. Did very well for her age. I rested today, washed many dishes, & froze corn.

Friday, July 22, 1977. Baby is talking in her bed at 10:15. Katie wants to close snaps on a slip & can't—fusses while I write! Mama stops & helps.

Saturday, July 23, 1977. I prepared picnic eats, then we went to school homecoming. Few of my schoolmates attended. Sunny & warm. After a program in P.M. some played ball. I did Saturday work in evening. Eli washed dishes.

Sunday, July 24, 1977. Rained on way to church at David Fishers. Eli Stolzfus of Pennsylvania preached deep sermon. Text: Luke 12 − 13. We were at Jacobs for supper & to Andy Bs for a singing in behalf of the Pennsylvania couples.

Monday, July 25, 1977. Northerly breeze. I did breakfast dishes of yesterday & today in A.M. & rocked my girlies. Was washing when Bertha and her sister and two sisters of Pennsylvania came along.

Tuesday, July 26, 1977. 70 in bedroom in morning. I got up b-4 the sun & folded wash, put them away & washed supper & lunch dishes of yesterday. Eli drove to work taking 5 doz. eggs @ $0.40 a doz. & large tomatoes to sell. Baby hit tomato gravy in my breakfast plate with full force! Ha.

Wednesday, July 27, 1977. Kayleen Shelter brought me 2 bushels of Sugar Dot sweet corn @ $3.50 a bushel. Nice corn. I worked up 1 3/4 bushels adding lima beans to one batch to freeze. Baby was rather fussy in P.M.

Thursday, July 28, 1977. Because I didn't get finished with my sweet corn yesterday, I finished it today, adding acid from the drug store that I ordered. Will this canned corn be better?

Friday, July 29, 1977. Vera's birthday anniversary marks 32. Eli went with Bill Benders to put up ESFs' tent last evening & left Katie at ESFs for the night, so today Barbara & I are alone. Warm day.

Saturday, July 30, 1977. Eli returned Katie in morning on spring wagon when he brought medicine for the chicks. Eli helped put up ESFs' tent in forenoon at Pine Ridge School for a school reunion today.

Sunday, July 31, 1977. Went to church at Amos Fishers for second time. Dan Bontrager chose to read I Cor. 13 after sermons. Katie fell from porch @ Amoses & hurt herself. Were @ ESFs for supper.

Monday, August 1, 1977. Eli's 2 weeks of paid vacation begins! In A.M. he attended road business & I washed. Emma Ruth got eggs in P.M. Their dog tagged along and got a ride home. He probably liked that.

Tuesday, August 2, 1977. Cool and cloudy. Our family went to Mark Fishers. That's different from most weekdays! Edna & Leah came, too. We dressed 20 fryers. Katie received a hard bump on forehead by landing on cement steps!

Wednesday, August 3, 1977. Quickly I stirred up a batch of grapenuts & we had warm grapenuts for breakfast. Eli crumbled the rest. I cleaned along walks and scratched [removed old finish in preparation for a fresh coat of paint] chest of drawers. Nice day.

Thursday, August 4, 1977. Eli knocked down the chimney which extended from roof. He met up with wasps but didn't get stung. I hoed in the garden and pulled kohlrabi which were so chewed up (leaves), woody, too.

Friday, August 5, 1977. Rainy. Eli got off at Marks & Katie wanted to too, but couldn't—tears. We went to EFMs where I was in charge of children & dinner while the others cleaned at David Fishers.

Saturday, August 6, 1977. Rain. I washed diapers and children's dresses. Eli shod Blackie with 1 old shoe and went to Ivans and picked tomatoes for me. Katie's face is discolored from her bad bump on Tuesday.

Sunday, August 7, 1977. Sunny and warm. We attended church at David Fishers held for my dad. Al Mast of Indiana were there. In P.M. we went to FBMs. Were invited to John Fishers for supper but went home.

Monday, August 8, 1977. Rain in A.M. Eli sawed up some trees along fence west of Bill Troyer house while Katie enjoyed picking off wild cherries & eating them. She likes being with Daddy. I washed & baked bread.

Tuesday, August 9, 1977. We had workday. ESFs, Dan Brennemans, & Sam Millers were here for dinner. Men put up new chimney. Vera brought many cucumbers. Some were canned today.

Wednesday, August 10, 1977. I canned pickles before we went to Dans to help get ready for church. Baby was fussy & I didn't get much done. Washed windows on outside. Katie enjoyed being there—swing ride & barnyard.

Thursday, August 11, 1977. Rained last night—cool house in morning. I felt tired. Eli helped Mark again in the structure of his lean-to cattle barn. I was @ FBMs with my girls. Katie enjoyed the Kalona Park.

Friday, August 12, 1977. Eli returned to Marks to help on his project. So that's the way his vacation is going—away from home again. Will husband ever be a home worker? I canned 24 qt. vegetable soup.

Saturday, August 13, 1977. I canned 9 qt. of tomato soup before breakfast. Eli baked 80 mincemeat cookies & made pretty noodles. I made ketchup & mowed a little in evening. It rained again. Grass is green again.

Sunday, August 14, 1977. Davids & Lloyd Bs both are on trips to Indiana and Pennsylvania, but we had 2 visiting ministers instead. We were to JSFs for supper honoring Susan.

Monday, August 15, 1977. My, my, a fussy baby and a late start on washing a big wash. Baby was held yesterday and wants to be held again today. She used to not act so on Mondays. Katie thought a kidney bean in the soup was a bug. I laughed.

Tuesday, August 16, 1977. Katie slept long and I got a good lick put in by ironing. Also washed & ironed caps. Had dumplings for supper.

Wednesday, August 17, 1977. Dear diary—I'm way behind. All of the past August is unwritten in here, but I do have notes handy. Baby dear has the cold. Katie is out playing with Brownie. Dad is at work. I'm making ketchup & baking bread. Nice day.

Thursday, August 19, 1977. Star of Bethlehems are blooming. A big amount of grapes were cut and juice was made until late. By working so late I thought of Mae Faye. Eli worked on Bontragers' new bench.

Friday, August 20, 1977. We got up too late & driver had to wait on us to go to Bontragers in Buchanan County. Lloyds, Jacobs, & Ray & Bertha went, too. We had a good dinner. Eli took their unfinished bench along & worked on it there.

Saturday, August 18, 1977. Nice day. Last evening on short notice for my part we went up to homeplace to see Norman Fishers of Ohio. Today I mowed lawn. Place does look better, of course.

Sunday, August 21, 1977. Last evening's supper & this morning's breakfast dishes remained unwashed. To Sunday School we went, not inviting anyone for dinner. Alas, home we come & company is here! What a surprise. They were outside eating their own food before going to see Ray.

Monday, August 22, 1977. I washed my many dirty dishes from Saturday morning on. Got a late start washing clothes. In P.M. I laid Barbara beside Katie in Katie's bed. Barbara opened her mouth & sang gurgles from her throat. When I'd left the room Katie laid on Barbara, so out goes baby.

Tuesday, August 23, 1977. After breakfast I fed chicks, giving Katie a ride on carrier. Willie's boys came for eggs. Baby wanted me, then Katie wanted to sit in my lap to look @ a bedtime storybook.

Wednesday, August 24, 1977. Eli came home with news. Luke (nephew) wants to be here overnight. He came on Jacob's cart and was here for supper & overnight. Katie gave him a goodnight kiss (tickled me).

Thursday, August 25, 1977. Busy mother about the place making ketchup, etc. In evening I was in such a hurry to go to Chesters that I didn't bother to put on shoes. I was the only woman barefoot! Sam Miller group had supper there.

Friday, August 26, 1977. I had so many tomatoes, I didn't know what to do, so I put them all together in one big blue (shoe?) no—canner (ha). And they scorched the bottom. My, my, my—how will they taste this winter?

Saturday, August 27, 1977. Nice day. Had another workday to get ready for the Fisher reunion. Men cut wood. Women cleaned, sewed, & removed black paint from that ol' chest of drawers. And we all ate dinner! (ha)

Sunday, August 28, 1977. Cloudy & rain. We attended church at Dan Brennemans in the buggy shed. Sermons by Joe and Sam Miller. I left baby's bib lay. We visited with Jonah Clara & girls on way home.

Monday, August 29, 1977. What a big wash! Did manage to get ironed & put clothes almost all away, but was a long day since I was up shortly after 4. Felt sleepy, too.

Tuesday, August 30, 1977. I got up about 4:00 & gathered curtains & put them in soak, red beets, too, & crawled back to bed! Edna canned 2 gal. & 2 qt. for me, Leah & I trimmed lawn. Katie & Fannie played.

Wednesday, August 31, 1977. Last day in August. Surely had a lot of rain this month. Mary Lou & Ann Marie were here to help get ready for reunion. We got a lot done. Baby was rather fussy. Had a stomach disorder.

5 Sarah the Entrepreneur:
The Fisher Kitchens

I decided to open up my table and put in the leaves. . . .
I never dreamed what would happen when we started baking.
Sarah Fisher

"I never dreamed what would happen when we began to bake. I baked myself right out of the house," Sarah said.

It all started with the Farmers' Market, where local vendors rent a space and sell their garden produce, home-baked goods, and homemade crafts. As the Fishers walked along, Sarah heard a man say that he wanted a black raspberry pie. She told me what followed: "It cost $6.00, but he didn't have that much money. He bought a rhubarb one, instead. It was less expensive, and he ate it all. This made me think. So I opened up my table and put in the leaves. I made rolls, bread, and rhubarb pie and went to the next week's Farmers' Market. She, the Market Master—notice it was a woman—wouldn't let us. We had to know the rules. She told us we had to pay for the stall and arrange for it in advance. She said she hoped to see us the next week."

The following week, Sarah and Eli made the arrangements. Rolls, a few pies, and a dozen loaves of bread "were gone in a hurry." Today, the Fisher Kitchens' baked goods are sold at several outlets: the Farmers' Market from May to October, and all year long at a local auction house and at a country store.

"I never dreamed what would happen when we started baking," Sarah said.

As the baking business grew, she found that "baking and living in the same house was just not possible." They needed space for racks to stack sixty pies and forty loaves of bread, room for the gas-powered mixing machines, and a place to wash and dry the multitude of baking dishes. The 1873, two-story farmhouse was not adequate for the family and the baking activities. So Eli built a new house with some assistance from relatives and friends.

In one diary entry, Sarah imagined her house in a remodeled state, and she added a speculative sketch labeled "subject to change." The sketch included a key with six items, notably a cooking stove, worktables, and a heater. Comparing the sketch to what was actually built, Sarah said, "It was a good start. We didn't end

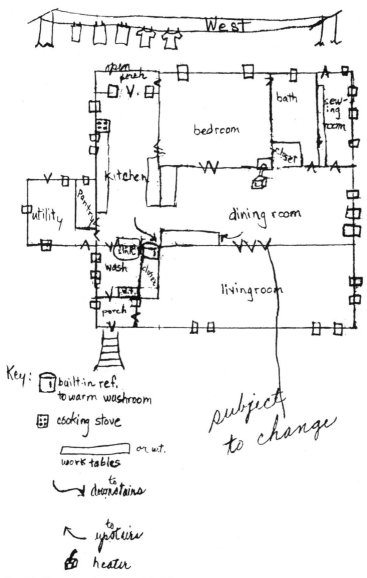

West

open porch

V.

bedroom

bath

sewing room

kitchen

closet

utility

Pantry

dining room

wash

E.H.R.

closet

wash

porch

living room

Key:
- built-in ref. to warm washroom
- cooking stove
- or w.t. work tables
- to downstairs
- to upstairs
- heater

subject to change

Sarah's diary sketch: a remodeled home.

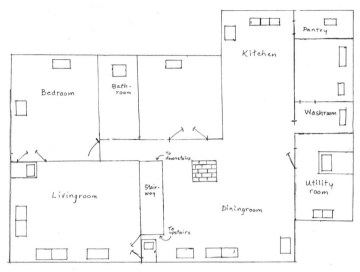

Sarah's sketch: the new house.

up remodeling. We decided to build a new house. Look how I set up the kitchen in the drawing compared to how it really is in the new house. We may brush on a coat of paint on the baking house. We want to fix it up a little so that it looks as good as the new house."

The new, two-story house is located just across the yard and separated from the old one by three clotheslines. Designed by Eli and Sarah together, the house is big enough to host church services for two hundred people. It was built primarily of recycled materials; woodwork out of the old house was installed in the new one, and beams used in the foundation were salvaged from a warehouse in Cedar Rapids. The windows and doors are positioned so that the maximum amount of natural light is available for sewing, cooking, and bookkeeping for the Fisher Kitchens. The driveway wraps around both houses, and the hitching post is next to the baking house. Loading outgoing baked goods and receiving incoming baking supplies are much easier now.

Bake Day

Every day except Sunday is what Sarah and her family call a bake day. I stood in the Fisher Kitchens, feeling the excitement of the atmosphere. Four hired girls, Eli, and Sarah were just beginning bake-day tasks. "What tools do you use?" I asked.

Sarah said, "The dough mixer, located in the former pantry, that is operated by a gas engine; a sheeter that rolls the dough into flat, rectangular sheets for various recipes, such as Danish or cinnamon rolls; the slicer for evenly sliced breads; the cake decorator tools because the cakes sell more readily if decorated; a scale so that we have a consistent quantity for bread loaves; the two ovens; six rolling pins; our hands; and our heads!" With that, Sarah plunged her fist into a huge, stainless-steel mixing bowl, combining the ingredients for pie dough.

At the same time, Eli was weighing dough for the bread loaves. He said to me, "Did you know that many of the English don't even know how to bake a pie?" I didn't tell Eli that my once-a-year Fourth of July blueberry pie takes me all of a day to bake.

One oven was set at 325 degrees for breads and one at 375 degrees for pies. Sarah has invented a way to bake nine pies at a time. They go in for fifteen minutes on the top shelf, and then fifteen minutes on the bottom. Six to ten loaves of bread go in the other gas oven. As I watched, a hired girl moved swiftly to one of the ovens and, with a few effortless motions, whisked nine pies past me and onto cooling racks. I could feel the heat on my face and quickly stepped aside. She carried the pies to the cooling and loading area, formerly the front porch.

Across the kitchen, Sarah stood before the stainless-steel bowl containing pie dough. "Here's how I make a fancy pie," she said, as she picked up two tools. One was a metal pastry cutter and the other a piece of another kitchen gadget that had come apart. Its rough edges could create a consistent, decorative edge when pressed on the pie-shell rim. Sarah deftly rolled out the dough, flipped it into the aluminum pie pan, and swiftly pressed one of the tools onto the edge of the shell. She rolled the top crust, made three marks together, and then three more. I saw the pattern of two flowers on the top crust. Sarah said, "Now, this is more interesting. They sell better this way, but this is also how I like to make them for our family."

Sarah the entrepreneur has expanded the family's world. On a weekly basis they visit with friends and relatives wherever they sell their goods. News of upcoming weddings, quiltings, and frolics (gatherings to accomplish specific tasks such as fence or barn building) are all part of the sale. The Fisher Kitchens' goods appear on a regular basis at their outlets. Someone must be at the Farmers' Market space each week because people expect it, and Sarah says this consistency is crucial to the success of their business. Their reputation is made of more than palatable products; they are known as honest people. The Fisher Kitchens have a faithful following in the non-Amish community. Eli told a story about fruit rolls and one weekly customer: "Sarah shapes the fruit rolls in loops to fancy them up, and this particular customer especially liked them for this reason. After the customer purchased several baked items, she arrived home to discover that she still owed five dollars. She came back to the Farmers' Market and tried to pay me the money."

Sarah ended the story with, "Eli refused to take the money, and, for the woman's honesty, he handed her *another* tray of fruit rolls!"

Another factor in the Fisher Kitchens' success is the calm, organized manner with which Eli presents the products. Anna Swartz and I viewed this firsthand when we attended one of the weekly auctions at which Eli sells baked goods. The frenzied pitch of the auction was in full swing when we arrived. The auctioneer was "crying" the sale, and the "spotters" were periodically shouting acknowledgment of the subtle bids back to him, selling everything from used cars to downhill skis.

Eli arrived at his regular time, about one hour after the sale started. Seeing him enter, at least twenty people rushed toward him. Money in hand, they followed him as he rolled in the still-warm blackberry pies, breads, and rolls. As he moved the goods across the auction floor, he patiently answered customers' questions: "Yes, we have cherry pie. No, there's no pumpkin this week." He took bills, made change, and handed out pies and plates of rolls. At the same time, he promoted a new item of the week: "Take a look. This week we have firewood for sale. My driver is bringing it in now."

I asked Sarah, "Can a woman set up a business on her own, or does it take both husband and wife? How difficult is it to get started?"

"I'm not in this alone," Sarah responded.

Sarah and Eli work collaboratively, but each focuses on specific aspects of the business. Sarah said, "We all have different talents and different natures. Eli enjoys doing comparing prices, finding the best buy, and ordering all the supplies. This summer we bought red raspberries for fifty dollars for thirty pounds locally. Now next year we'll have more of our own and probably won't have to buy them. We use our own blackberries. We use what we have if we can. Eli drives the baked goods to the store in the buggy, and hires a driver to go to the Farmers' Market and the auction. Eli is our main seller. I do most of the baking along with the hired girls, and we both go over the bookkeeping together. It just depends on what you like to do. It's a cooperative effort with us."

In order to keep a consistent baking schedule and products, Sarah hires and trains girls from her community to assist in the Kitchens. Sarah said this is one of the biggest challenges. Three recently ended their employment when they accepted teaching positions in the Amish schools. Often, one hired girl helps train her sister, who then takes her place.

During bake day at the Fisher Kitchens, I viewed a microcosm of the business world. Sarah was the personnel manager, quality control, expert market analyst, cost analyst, bookkeeper, and crew boss. I learned that Sarah's products are not the plain fare I had anticipated. Instead they are creatively designed pies, rolls, and breads baked in response to the marketplace.

Sarah had actually been an entrepreneur for some time. While writing her diary, she managed the household and cared for "two diaper babies" (her term for two babies in the diaper stage at the same time). She also prepared for church services in her home for two hundred people, tended her garden, and participated in community events such as quiltings. All this prepared her for her entrepreneurial role. She said, "After all, I have baked in large quantities for a long time."

THE FISHER KITCHENS' BLACKBERRY PIE

Sarah multiplies the following recipe by three and makes several such batches each bake day.

CRUST FOR PIE
3 cups flour
1 teaspoon salt
1 cup shortening (1/2 lard and 1/2 Crisco, or all lard)
1/4 cup milk
1/4 cup water
1/4 cup oil

Makes 5 crusts (nine-inch size) for any kind of pie. Can be frozen in advance of using.

BLACKBERRY PIE FILLING
3/4 to 1 cup sugar
3 tablespoons cornstarch
1/2 teaspoon salt
1/4 cup water
4 cups blackberries
1 tablespoon butter
1 tablespoon lemon juice

Combine first 4 ingredients and 2 of the 4 cups of berries. Boil until thick and clear. Stir in lemon juice and butter. Place the remaining 2 cups of berries in the pie shell. Top with the cooked mixture. May be served with whipped cream on top instead of a pie crust top.

September and October 1976

Wednesday, September 1, 1976. Cool & cloudy. I finished Katie's aqua dress & made her a cap & sewed together a royal blue sweater that I'd cut last week from a pullover sweater (a discard).

Thursday, September 2, 1976. Pretty day. Katie is out in the playpen south of house under maple tree (P.M.). She talks & entertains herself. I canned 6 qt. peaches & made a big, big batch of ketchup.

Friday, September 3, 1976. Nice morning. Shortly after 8:00 A.M. Jonah Fisher picked us up & we 3 with Emmanuel & Hattie & Bertha were Indiana bound. Had good luck all the way. Katie behaved well. We were at Bontragers overnight.

Saturday, September 4, 1976. Jonah took us to the wedding of cousin Lydie Stolfus & Michael John Schmucker in Michigan. Katie was very ill-behaved during services. Had good eats at reception. Visited, then went to Robert Rosettas for the night.

Sunday, September 5, 1976. We were in church at Robert Ts where baptismal services were held. Had supper.

Monday, September 6, 1976. We were at Dale Hs last night & this morning for breakfast of pancakes & sausage. We were at Chester Mae's store where we bought a gray double-knit remnant, at A. Millers for dinner, and back to Bontragers for the night. Had ice cream in evening & visitors.

Tuesday, September 7, 1976. After breakfast we started for home stopping first at Charles Benders, got Emmanuel Johns at Neal Fishers & headed on. Dads were with us. Came home safely about 4:20. Katie stood the trip well, having fun with Emmanuel Hattie & sleeping.

Wednesday, September 8, 1976. Our little Betz! Today I asked her how the puppy makes and she barked, "Uh,uh,uh." I washed twice today and ironed.

Thursday, September 9, 1976. Mrs. Dale Fisher called for a doz. eggs. We sell them at $0.40 a doz. I mowed lawn and canned grape juice. Nice day.

Friday, September 10, 1976. I brought in from the garden: cabbages, carrots, Chieftain potatoes, gladiola bulbs, beans, and hoed. Eli tilled in the garden & I pulled out tomato plants in the evening. We had peach cobbler for supper.

Saturday, September 11, 1976. Eli worked in A.M. and came home for a late dinner. I shelled ground cherries and canned more grape juice.

Sunday, September 12, 1976. We attended the Vernon Benders church district. We were at ESFs for supper.

Monday, September 13, 1976. The exhaust pipe leaks in basement so I couldn't wash. My yeast was almost all gone so I couldn't bake. So I patched socks & cut & sewed a dress for Katie.

Tuesday, September 14, 1976. I stacked my breakfast dishes and leaving Eli at work we 2 rode on to Kalona for a quilting at Lois's. I had a lot of business in town in A.M. Had delicious food at Lois's.

Wednesday, September 15, 1976. Until I had my many dishes washed from yesterday & this morning, it was late when I began my washing. I did manage to get most of it folded & put away, though.

Thursday, September 16, 1976. Our plastic tray for the high chair is broken so we push Missie up to the table. This morning she climbed from it onto the table! We went to a quilting at Merle Waglers.

Friday, September 17, 1976. I baked bread, rolls, & fried doughnuts, made carrot salad, & canned tomato chunks & juice. Katie pulled loose the curtain holder & stuck the nail in her mouth! Mama found it before she swallowed it.

Saturday, September 18, 1976. Our Missie has her way of saying, "cracker." I baked 4 ground-cherry pies & cleaned. In P.M. Eli & I swept the Sunday School house.

Sunday, September 19, 1976. (Our second anniversary) After Sunday School, Lloyds, Joes, and Jacobs were here for dinner. It rained in the A.M. Sunday School lessons: Acts 8. Attendance: 142.

Monday, September 20, 1976. Cloudy at first but the sun broke through in A.M. I picked red Delicious apples, approximately 4 bushels, & brought in the last grapes & canned 2 qt. of juice. The sparrows got their share evidently as many were gone. Katie tore the shade in her room.

Tuesday, September 21, 1976. Very windy from the north which made the wash flutter. I had the heater a-going in the kitchen, but turned it off in the evening. I folded wash, put away practically all, & ironed. We sold $4.00 worth of apples in evening or 1 bushel & 10 1/2 lb.

Wednesday, September 22, 1976. This is bake & make day. I began baking cookies at about 4:45 A.M. (couldn't sleep anyhow). I made over 100 cookies, 8 loaves of bread, lime cabbage salad, & potato-macaroni salad, & 2 pumpkin pies.

Thursday, September 23, 1976. Ray came in A.M. and was here helping pick our apples and snapped popcorn. I picked up apples from the ground and sorted & wrapped some. Our apples are blemishy & few.

Friday, September 24, 1976. We had soft-boiled eggs, fried mush & liverwurst for breakfast. Ray really ate. He finished snapping popcorn and dug potatoes & shucked some popcorn. He gave us a big lift. I sorted apples & washed spuds.

Saturday, September 25, 1976. Rainy. We went to the funeral of Susan Hochstetler who died of pneumonia. Indiana friends attended. We shopped in Kalona afterwards getting Katie a size 3 blanket sleeper, etc., then went to Andy Ropps' sale.

Sunday, September 26, 1976. Cloudy all day. Rained last night. We were at Sunday School, then to Luke Gingeriches for dinner. In evening Emmanuel Ina & we visited Bills & Mary.

Monday, September 27, 1976. Cloudy most all day. Rained slightly in A.M. I shucked 1 bushel of yellow popcorn and made Katie 1 everyday brown dress. Eli & I stripped cane by lantern light after supper [removed the portion of the plant that will be processed into molasses].

Tuesday, September 28, 1976. Had a late start in washing & many diapers. Weather was cloudy so the trousers didn't dry. Joni Fishers all helped strip cane in evening. Eli was very glad the stripping's done.

Wednesday, September 29, 1976. Ann Marie had 30 old hens to butcher. Katie and I went. Mae Faye & Vera helped, too. In evening we went to ESFs. Eli helped process cane. I helped with supper.

Thursday, September 30, 1976. Pretty day. Bertha was here and dug Mom's sweet potatoes that I had planted for her. After I had dressed & butchered 10 fryers, she delivered them to Gingerich Implement via home. Eli loaded cane.

Friday, October 1, 1976. Very warm! Eli beheaded 20 fryers in morning & I dressed them, keeping 1. Also sold 6 liveweight in evening. Eli rode to ESFs with Peter Troyer who hauled the cane & forgot to unload the cans! Forgetful Daddy. So Peter took them back down after he had been home.

Saturday, October 2, 1976. About 7:30 A.M. a large wedge of wild geese winged over our home, their light plumage reflecting the sun's brilliance. I cold packed 14 qt. of tomatoes & made 5 qt. of juice. In P.M. I went to get Eli who had stayed at ESFs last evening to help with the sorghum.

Sunday, October 3, 1976. We attended baptismal services for James

Miller and Ruby Borkholder at Levi Millers. Were at FBMs for supper.

Monday, October 4, 1976. Now one year old is our little "Miss" who is not aware of it. Mama gave her a piggy bank, and she liked it. She said in her way, "I piggy." I washed. In P.M. I made 2 pumpkin pies & roasted a fryer.

Tuesday, October 5, 1976. I dressed 12 fryers & put them in refrigerator for tomorrow's order. In P.M. I widened Katie's 2 brown skirts that I had to narrow when I made her dresses. Katie walked by herself in evening. I ironed while Eli washed supper dishes.

Wednesday, October 6, 1976. First hard frost. Up and at it! We plucked 13 fryers before breakfast. I dressed them and really hurried. Was done & ready to go help Vera by about 11:15. There we also dressed chickens. Ann & Susan were there, too. I sold 25 fryers in evening for $11.50.

Thursday, October 7, 1976. Seven loaves of bread were baked in our kitchen, 1 dress cut & sewed together for Katie, lamps filled, flowerslips brought in & a little mending done. I made a mixture of lard & sulphur & applied some on Missie's ouchy bottom.

Friday, October 8, 1976. Second hard frost. Katie is better. I dressed & cut up 4 chickens. The one was a pullet that had its tail chewed up & was hurt by the enemy under the eye last night [an intruder such as a fox or owl]. Eli had forgotten to close the door!

Saturday, October 9, 1976. Eli set up the stove in living room b-4 breakfast. Sunny & nice morning. I brought in cabbages & white potatoes from the mulch patch. Have some very nice ones. Also husked popcorn that had been setting in the bag by the row, unseen.

Sunday, October 10, 1976. Church @ Bill Masts. Had Romans 12. Honey & tomatoes to eat. Wanda & Dan were published [upcoming wedding was announced].

Monday, October 11, 1976. The Lord is so good to us. He gave me strength to wash, iron, and patch today. We have much to be thankful for—food, clothing shelter, relaxation in sleeping instead of fear of the enemy.

Tuesday, October 12, 1976. To ESFs we go—Katie & I. In the A.M. I helped strip cane & put a hem on Fannie's aqua suit for the wedding & patched 2 garments. They didn't cook today but with all the help others gave, the cane patch was finished.

Wednesday, October 13, 1976. I potted house plants—coleus, begonia, Star of Bethlehem roots, ivy, & philodendrons. A batch of hard crinkly gingersnaps & apple pies were baked. We had 1 small pie for supper. The 2 others will go for tomorrow's lunch. I also canned 15 qt. red beets.

Thursday, October 14, 1976. Nice day. I finished digging the Kennebecs. From 3 rows we got 3 bushels & better. I washed them & carried them downstairs save 3 which were unusual ones. One weighed 1 lb., 6 oz., and 2 others resembled animals! Also dug the sweet potatoes (very tired me).

Friday, October 15, 1976. To Kalona Katie & I go. Stopped for 1 bushel pears @ Isaac Ts & canned them (all but 1) yet in evening. Got 14 qts. with pineapple added to 5 qt.

Saturday, October 16, 1976. Eli returned from an all night's job cooking molasses @ ESFs. He ate breakfast & hitchhiked to Gingerich Implement to work! I picked him up about noon. We went to Ivan Fishers' sale. Ate early supper, then Eli slept on couch while Katie who had joined him for fun fell hard.

Sunday, October 17, 1976. Sunday School. Attendance: 132. Katie for the first time turned a picture of a dog around as it was upside down in Sunday School.

Monday, October 18, 1976. Eli beheaded 18 fryers & helped pluck them b-4 breakfast. Katie behaved so well that I had dressed them all before 1:30 P.M. I pieced a Lone Star quilt for Katie's bed.

Tuesday, October 19, 1976. Breakfast past—Eli gone to job—dishes unwashed. Bread rising & plum butter begun. Katie is helping herself to worktable drawers. Rags were dropped, diapers taken out & examined. Finally she pinched her fingers which brought Mama to action & tools & rags returned.

Wednesday, October 20, 1976. I helped Mae Faye get ready for church by cleaning [lantern] shades, also patched clothes. Katie & Vesta played nicely for the most part. I got home late. Eli was home from work and had brought in the wash for me.

Thursday, October 21, 1976. My Sunday medium blue dress and apron both were enlarged and lengthened. While I was sewing Katie reached in & got her soft patty in the wheel. Tears—but little harm. Into the playpen Mama put her where she was safer.

Friday, October 22, 1976. Mama [Sarah refers to self] had an appointment with Dr. Ballter @ 10:45 but she was late about 3/4 hour but still got in. I was at FBMs for dinner and P.M. Had left Katie in Grandma's care while I went uptown. Got squash in evening on way home.

Saturday, October 23, 1976. Eli & I cut out the styrofoam blocks for Wanda's wedding corner [display area], packed dishes, and took them along to ESFs. We helped get ready for the wedding. I dug carrots in P.M. Others set table(s).

Sunday, October 24, 1976. Cloudy. We went to Ed Yoders for church. T. J. Yoder preached the main sermon.

Monday, October 25, 1976. Up and at it! Eli helped me get started with the washing before breakfast. He made breakfast. I worked on the books for the wedding table and had quite a time of it. In evening I folded wash and ironed.

Tuesday, October 26, 1976. I left Katie at Larry Benders and went to ESFs to help get ready for the wedding. Grace Miller and I made 25 apricot pies for the occasion. Cakes were frosted and more tables set, etc.

Sarah doesn't throw things away. These machinery parts will come in handy when Eli or someone else needs to fix something.

Wednesday, October 27, 1976. Nice, sunny, chilly. Katie is walking around in house this morning and gets into mischief. She pulled some books from the bookshelf and quite enjoyed dumping clothes on the floor from the small chest of drawers. Mamma noticed her quietness so investigated!

Thursday, October 28, 1976. The wedding day came which made Dan and Wanda man & wife. I was cook. We had many guests & plenty of food. Approximately 215 dined @ dinner with extras included.

Friday, October 29, 1976. I sewed Katie & me each a white Sunday cap & cleaned & pressed my royal blue suit that I wore yesterday. In the evening we had a Sam Miller gathering @ Michael Ts. We sang & ate ice cream & cake left over from the wedding.

Saturday, October 30, 1976. Eli went to work in A.M. After morning duties I drove Blackie up to Sunday School & waited on him. Then we rode to Paul Yoders. Eli helped with carpenter work. Were there for dinner.

Sunday, October 31, 1976. To Sunday School and Bill Ts. Katie was fussy. Bills were there.

September and October 1977

Thursday, September 1, 1977. Neighbors Rebecca B, Dorothy Y. & Lettie Miller helped do a lot of work by washing windows & lamps, cleaning upstairs, baking angelfood cake, ironing, & trimming along walk & barn. I supervised, etc.

Friday, September 2, 1977. I thought work went slow in A.M. I cleaned up wash house & mowed. Edna Leah came in the P.M. & cleaned this and that. Tomorrow is the big day—Fisher reunion.

Saturday, September 3, 1977. We had a lot of people here for the Fisher reunion with a basket dinner under the big tent belonging to ESF. We had a program in P.M. It rained after 4 & came in through tent.

Sunday, September 4, 1977. We went to Sunday School. Had 10 youth here for a waffle dinner, a small crowd. Girls visited & 6 boys pitched horse shoes. In evening we had a good singing. Guests from Kentucky were here.

Monday, September 5, 1977. Labor Day. My husband helped me by hanging up wash. In P.M. he fixed torn window ropes. I folded wash and took care of the children. Eli went to Grace's store in evening.

Tuesday, September 6, 1977. Nice day. I baked 28 loaves of bread for gma, ironed, & hoed. The new neighbor's wife was here in P.M. to get acquainted.

Wednesday, September 7, 1977. Cloudy in morning but sun came out & dried off ground. I hoed & hauled weeds away, gathered ground cherries, downed sunflowers, & pulled out soybeans. My 3 sisters came & canned tomato juice, grape jelly, & made Barbara a cap. Katie says sentences now.

Thursday, September 8, 1977. Vera baked ginger cookies for church & washed & hung out diapers. Susan finished my hoeing & cleaned the strawberry patch. I supervised, etc. Susan picked large lima beans in P.M. Sunny & warm.

Friday, September 9, 1977. Erma came to help. We made 6 pies, 3 of each, apple & ground cherry. In evening we had a supper here with 5 couples attending. I really worked fast to get ready.

Saturday, September 10, 1977. Eli went to town in A.M. to buy brown bread for church & other supplies. I mopped and waxed kitchen and cleaned otherwise. 'Twas late when we got to bed.

Sunday, September 11, 1977. We had a beautiful day for church services outdoors under the tent with Eli Hershberger preaching main part & Emery Fisher reading text. Both are of Indiana. Approximately 130 people ate 4 gallons of pickles & about 35 loaves of bread. Very tired legs of mine.

Monday, September 12, 1977. Almost an all day rain & about an all day wash! I strung up lines under the tent & hung out diapers, etc. Left them out overnight. In basement I hung up dresses, etc. Didn't get to washing dishes until evening.

Tuesday, September 13, 1977. Cloudy most of day. We had the sewing with good attendance. I hung out wash in P.M. Women quilted downstairs by lamplight. We had 3 machines a-going.

Wednesday, September 14, 1977. Cool & sunny in morning. Katie was extra hungry since she had no supper. Barbara worked her way out from living room to kitchen. Baby holds milk bottle herself now.

Thursday, September 15, 1977. Dad & Bertha came. Bertha brought my cap she'd made for me & fixed the girlies' caps that she'd made, too. I packed some clothes in suitcase. In evening we went to hospital to see Al King of Buchanan County. It rained.

Friday, September 16, 1977. What on earth! Here comes our driver to take us to Joes in Missouri & we are not ready! Dear, dear! I understood 7 o'clock instead of 5!! Had dinner with Lyn & Lillian & supper at Joes.

Saturday, September 17, 1977. Green and warm today. Eli and Lloyd fished before dinner. Ann Marie & I ironed. In P.M. we went visiting with John Hochstetler our driver. Were at Amos Hochstetlers for supper.

Sunday, September 18, 1977. Church was at Dale Benders near neighbors of Joes. They had a singing in P.M.

Monday, September 19, 1977. Left Missouri, @ Joes about 9 A.M. & entered Kalona almost 4:30 P.M. Barbara slept in rear of van on a floor bed about 3 hours. Katie soon slept in her bed. Baby is now in jumper. She has a mad crying spell. Was spoiled by being held so much.

Tuesday, September 20, 1977. Pretty day. Sunny. I washed & ironed most of the ironing. The Lifetime Salesman [cookware salesman] brought our set costing us $229.60 with our other Volrath set traded in & some other deductions [Sarah values high-quality cookware for daily cooking needs and canning].

Wednesday, September 21, 1977. Cloudy—about 56 in morning. I put $141.34 in mail for Kalona Savings Bank, Eli's check for last week. Made a royal blue dress for Barbara & ironed it & hankies.

Thursday, September 22, 1977. Cloudy—64. Time, 8:40 A.M. Mae Annie & Vesta came. Mae Annie baked cookies & cleaned drawers. Vesta sang "Glory" repeatedly. I made 2 batches bread.

Friday, September 23, 1977. Cloudy & rainy. Susan & Ann Marie & Miriam F. were helpers today. Ann Marie pressed Eli's Sunday pants. Susan & Miriam cleaned cupboards. I baked 2 batches bread & supervised!

Saturday, September 24, 1977. Beautiful day! Eli is still mowing. Katie went home with Leah overnight. Ellen N. helped me today. It's shortly past 5:30 P.M. We set the table on north porch for to-morrow, cleaned, & baked 3 [picture of a cherry] pies.

Sunday, September 25, 1977. We had Council meeting here in our basement. Lloyd preached main sermon. Cousin Rebecca & Miriam F. waited on tables on north porch & in kitchen. 12 loaves of bread were left. Had 37.

Monday, September 26, 1977. Very nice wash day. 3 parties bought 37 of our young roosters at $0.80 apiece. I folded & put away wash and washed dishes, also put Sunday dishes used yesterday away.

Tuesday, September 27, 1977. Beautiful morning—fresh. I gave Barbara her first braids. I washed our buggy & ironed. Pennsylvania relatives visited in A.M.

Wednesday, September 28, 1977. At long last I made a seat for baby stroller from naugahyde, stripped cane, & dug potatoes. 2 snakes were in the patch, too. I killed the one—ugh, snakes! We've got them!

Thursday, September 29, 1977. Very cloudy overhead b-4 breakfast, but in P.M., sunny and beautiful. In A.M. I dressed 10 young roosters for Joes. Children slept well in A.M. which helped. Barbara pulled herself up on feet for first time. Katie set dinner table.

Friday, September 30, 1977. Guess where my daughters & I went today! To ESFs. Hadn't been there all spring or summer during the week for myself. They're cooking cane molasses. I washed dishes and made dumplings for a surprise.

Saturday, October 1, 1977. Cool, cloudy. Had rain during night. After Eli had left for work, I fed the 1400 pullets with both girls along. Katie held Barbara in the litter carrier while I finished feeding! Ray came & helped strip cane. My late cucumbers are bearing.

Sunday, October 2, 1977. Sunny & nice but rather breezy. We had fast day. Ray & Katie ate breakfast. Had Sunday School in P.M. We went on a wild goose chase to Jacobs, but the geese were gone so we returned home!

Monday, October 3, 1977. Very nice wash day with scores of diapers.

I folded most of it and put it away. I discovered Katie's new cuspid on the upper left. Baby enjoys the outdoors in the stroller.

Tuesday, October 4, 1977. Sunny in A.M. Cloudy in P.M. & a little rain at chore time. Katie showed Mama a live mouse holding it by the tail on her second birthday. I gathered ground cherries & kidney beans. Barbara was good in P.M.

Wednesday, October 5, 1977. Cloudy in morning, northwest wind. I'm canning 4 qts. cukes from my patch I started the last part of July. My first patch was poor.

Thursday, October 6, 1977. Nice day. I felt aching today—rather. Outdoors in the sunshine baby, Katie, & I breathed in fresh air as I plucked lima beans from the pulled plants. In P.M. Katie helped me shell them.

Friday, October 7, 1977. Eli had a sick spell last night. In morning I chored, made phone calls, & got a bushel of pears at Isaac Ts. In the rain we drove to Lloyds. I helped get ready for gma. Eli was at home.

Saturday, October 8, 1977. Cloudy & chilly. Sale today at John Fishers. We didn't go. Eli is at home from work. He's better. I milked Marigold in morning & carried the milk to Lloyds staying to wash windows. In P.M. I canned 14 qt. pears & cleaned here.

Sunday, October 9, 1977. Sunny but chilly wind. We walked & ran to church at James Bs. Katie wore black hose for first time. We had Communion services. In evening ESFs came.

Monday, October 10, 1977. Nice wash day in A.M. South wind. Barbara likes to play with the sewing machine treadle, & crawls, & babbles. So cute & sweet child! Blessing from God. Katie shelled kidney beans.

Tuesday, October 11, 1977. Cloudy, chilling wind. After feeding the pullets and getting the girls & myself ready we were off with our neighbor to a Sarah quilting at Bill Hochstetlers. Had delicious food.

Wednesday, October 12, 1977. Today is the funeral of little Dorothy S., daughter of Richard Ss. Poor child on earth, but a "blossom" in heaven. I canned 3 qt. pears and baked bread, also gathered walnuts.

Thursday, October 13, 1977. Beautiful October weather. Sisters Bertha & Ann Marie & Mae & Susan were here to see Mae who didn't show up! We ate & visited. Ann Marie & I dug carrots & stripped cane. Nice evening—stars shining & Eli & I worked in cane patch.

Friday, October 14, 1977. October's bright blue weather—beautiful! 80. A huge flock of honking geese winged southward after dinner. The call of the wild—exciting. I dug potatoes & stripped cane.

Saturday, October 15, 1977. While doing supper dishes yesterday evening, Katie wanted to wipe, so I let her. She stood on the little bench with a big red tea towel in her hand & sort of dried glasses! (ha) Ann Marie came to help strip cane. We got it done! Cane was at ESFs by evening.

Sunday, October 16, 1977. We attended Sunday School & had dinner at Brother Jacobs. Mae babysat for us while we went to John Fishers in double buggy. Scenery colorful with pheasants on the wing. Autumn.

Monday, October 17, 1977. I washed, folded, & ironed clothes. Eli brought home our molasses in evening of 15 gallons which is about half as much as last year. I gave Barbara her last nursing of what little there was!

Tuesday, October 18, 1977. I dug potatoes & bought cheese from Glen Leigh & picked kidney beans. Katie helped pick up apples & fell on garden cart cutting a gash in her head. We made cider in evening at Amos Fishers.

Wednesday, October 19, 1977. Very nice. Keith Byler of Ottumwa got pullets. The little girls were out too & watched. I helped by handing chicks to Keith from Eli. In A.M. I canned apple cider.

Thursday, October 20, 1977. Very nice outdoors. I baked bread and whole wheat gingersnap cookies. Alice got 1/2 gallon of molasses & borrowed stepladder. In evening I chopped off Star of Bethlehem plants. Girls were out, too.

Friday, October 21, 1977. Sunny and very warm. I even bathed Katie out on south porch! In A.M. we worked in garden. Katie & I gathered green peppers, cabbage, and lima beans. In evening we went to Sam Millers' 49th anniversary supper at H. Masts. Had oyster soup, salads, celery, pie, & ice cream.

Saturday, October 22, 1977. Cloudy all day. Chilly. Eli went to work and was home for a late dinner. Dan B. brought supplies for his new buggy Eli is to make. Barbara has a sore throat. Katie rode on Daddy's lap on cart to deliver molasses. I prepared food and cleaned.

Sunday, October 23, 1977. Rainy morning. We rode to church @ Lloyds. Women put on wraps to go from big house to Lloyds' little house after church. Herman B. fell from haymow on cement floor.

Monday, October 24, 1977. Cloudy & more rain in A.M. I set out my Giant Robinson strawberry plants and washed in P.M. Some of the diapers were dry enough to fold. Others were folded & put in oven overnight.

Tuesday, October 25, 1977. I cut some bibs for baby & made 1, the other almost. My dad came at noon. Was here for dinner and sorted soybeans in P.M., then went on up to Emmanuel Johns for supper. Damp & cloudy.

Wednesday, October 26, 1977. Sunny & pretty day. Katie, Barbara, & I went to the sewing at Larry B. Millers. On way home both girls slept. I folded wash in evening that I'd hung out in morning before leaving. (Finished bib in morning b-4 going to sewing & took it along).

Thursday, October 27, 1977. Beautiful day. I got tomato racks out of the garden and washed out diapers. With husband gone so much I don't have much ambition to work. Dan Brennemans brought us 39 brown pullets in evening.

Friday, October 28, 1977. I baked 8 loaves of bread & canned 12 qt. pears. In evening we had hamburger & pear gravy & fresh brown & white bread. Went to ESFs to pay $3,000 on principal, then to Sam Millers. David Millers of Illinois were there visiting.

Saturday, October 29, 1977. In A.M. Katie & Barbara & I were all outdoors. I raked leaves in lawn from big maple & spread them on garden, made simple twine swing for Katie & put screen on wash house door replacing the torn plastic one. Eli worked in A.M. & was @ ESFs in P.M. working on their John Deere.

Sunday, October 30, 1977. Cloudy all day. Trees have lost much beauty since 2 weeks ago when we drove to Wellman. Good thing we went then. We went to Sunday School in A.M., & then to Mother's grave afterwards. Then were home for rest of day. I began looking at Mom's get well mail. [picture of eyes] Very tired.

Monday, October 31, 1977. To Eli's disappointment it was raining this morning. He had wanted to plow the garden. Cloudy all day. My girls & I went to Lloyds. I helped butcher old hens. Mae Faye was there, too. Bertha & Dad came & were supper & overnight guests.

6 Sarah the Writer: Circle Letters and Poetry

I've ended my diary keeping, but I've started writing more circle letters right here at this table.
Sarah Fisher

Sarah and I were hulling strawberries at our usual place, the picnic table under the maple tree. Before us sat twenty-five pint containers of Cardinal strawberries so large that a single berry filled a quarter cup measure. Removing the hulls was the first step in the canning process, and it gave us time to sit, think, and occasionally talk. I thought about how Sarah and her family would eat the strawberries all winter long. I felt rich with news and knowledge of Sarah's life. I asked, "Sarah, do you still keep a diary?"

Sarah said, "No, when the children were very young, I enjoyed keeping a diary, but I wouldn't get as much satisfaction from it now. I'm busy with the baking business and gardening. I've ended my diary keeping, but I've started writing more circle letters. When the envelope of letters comes, I take out my old letter and put in a new one. They give me my history instead of a diary. It's a record for my family of our activities."

Sarah explained that an Amish circle letter is started by one person who lists six to ten other writers, writes a letter, places it in a large envelope, and sends it on to the next person on the list to add a letter and so on. The circle letter packet comes back to the beginning and starts over. When Sarah receives the envelope, she removes her old letter, inserts her new one, and sends the packet on to the next person. Sarah said, "This way, the circle letter never ends."

Sarah writes several circle letters per month. She said, "We group ourselves according to some commonality." She calls one her Friendship Circle, a letter started with friends when she was fifteen. She also belongs to a circle of women born the same year and a circle of cousins. One of Sarah's friends is in a circle of women named Rachel, and one belongs to a group of eight women whose birthday is the same year. Teacher circle writers describe ideas, such as a new way to organize a spelling bee, or they might tell what foods were brought by the parents to the last day's picnic. Sarah said a teacher she knows is in a circle with teachers from

Amish communities in Canada and the United States. Sarah said, "It's a variety pack. They're from all over."

Any special instructions, like the time limit on holding the circle letters, are included on the cover list of names. Usually a turnaround time of five to seven days is allowed, after which the writer must pay a fine of several cents. The group may decide to drop a consistently tardy writer altogether. Other times, participants drop out, and new members are added.

I thought of the dreadful form letters I receive that are sent to everyone on a person's Christmas card list. I asked Sarah, "Isn't it hard to write to a group? Does it make the letter very general? How would you specifically ask someone a question?"

Sarah said, "We write to a manageable number of people, and everyone expects and receives a response." She said she likes to write about ordinary things, like the flicker that built a nest in the trees next to the garden or about events such as weddings and births. Sarah explained that each person listed writes his or her number at the top of the letter and then signs it.

"You always know who is writing what," she said. If the writer wants to ask a question she might write, "Number 3, what new things have you planted in your garden this year?" To begin, the writer might start with "Dear Readers," or "Dear Friends," or "Dear Cousins." According to Sarah, "You simply write like you talk in a conversation and everyone writes back."

Sarah went to a drawer in her sideboard that stores her dishes and pulled out a box. "I save letters for each child. I call it my sunshine box. This is a letter from one of my friends. She talked to me in her letter about so many things. Recently, when I had a lot of work to get done, I read her letter over again and felt better. That's why it's called the sunshine box. Here, take a look." I picked up the handwritten letter and began to read:

March 22

Dear Friends,

Greetings in Jesus' High & Holy Name! This leaves me on a Sunday, P.M., just got home from church.

Do any of you cook maple syrup? We have cooked 82 gallons from the first run. Have still a couple hundred gallons of sap that isn't cooked.

John had planned to serve dinner down in the woods for the school this week. But with the cold weather coming in they gave it up.

Is chore time so will close. Wishing you all the best.

Mary

Sarah said, "Now, you see, that's how I do circle letters and why I save them. But we are part of different worlds. It's time for you to start a circle letter on your own." So I did. I started a teacher circle letter with my college students in teacher preparation and with teachers I knew in rural schools in South Dakota and West Virginia. College student Tessa wrote the first letter:

April 10

Dear Friends,

I've come up with some very exciting new ideas for my sixth grade language group. I've decided to do a lesson on circle letter writing. I think the children will love this! Don't you? #2: How are your plans coming along for your group? #1: Have you gone to the Iowa store in the mall to see if they have any more books on Iowa history?

Until next time,
Tessa

Sarah said, "It sounds a lot like how our teachers write to each other. A teacher I know is in a circle with Amish teachers from Midwestern states. They compare what they are doing in school." Then, in her dialect, Sarah asked her daughter Mary a question. "I asked her to bring something out for us," she said. Mary went into the house and came back with a vintage train case, trimmed in tobacco brown and covered in a cream-and-brown herringbone pattern. Sarah placed it on the picnic table between us. We continued to talk about the height of the corn and the number of two quart jars necessary to can the berries. Finally, I couldn't wait any longer.

"Is there something in the suitcase?" I asked.

"I have something to show you," Sarah said. We both laughed. "Open it up."

Suddenly, I imagined that the humid wind coming off the cornfield was a salt breeze on a sultry beach, the unlatching of the case was the lifting of a treasure chest's massive trunk lid. I unsnapped it and looked inside. I didn't find gold. But what I found was indeed priceless—pages and pages of poems on neatly folded notebook paper written in the even handwriting I had come to know so well.

"Besides letters, I write poetry as the mood strikes," Sarah said. The first poem we read was one she had written as an eleven-year-old in school. Sarah had not met the deadline for completing the poem, so at the last minute she wrote the following:

A poem, a poem(!)
Oh, what could it be!
It's class period already
Oh, mercy me!
Shall it be of hills or of valleys and plains?
Or of man sick with pills and pains?
I think I shall settle on neither of these.
Instead I shall tell of Swiss cheese.
This cheese is so odd with many a hole
Which vary in size from a pen to a mole.
From a day's work at school plodding hungrily you come.
Swiss cheese and crackers serve best for a bum!

Sarah then read aloud a poem she had written as an adult. It stays safely within the rules and boundaries of traditional poetry and expresses themes identified by Doug Kachel in his essay "The Memoriam Poetry of the Old Order Amish." Most focus on the writer's feelings about the loss of a loved one and religious convictions about life after death.

KIND GRANDMA

Grandmother is only 56,
But yet she goes out to gather sticks,
Mornings she milks the 2 red kine [cows],
Then she feeds the 4 brown swine.

She'd often have children in her lap,
When they'd want down, she'd give them a tap.
Grandmother is not selfish but she is kind,
Nevertheless she has a good mind.

But once Grandmother was not old,
Oft her childhood she'd foretold
Of how they usually had such fun
By playing games with everyone.

Grandmother fell asleep at 97.
She had gone to live with the angels in heaven.
"We shall miss kind Grandmother, dear,"
Would say the children with a tear.

Later I shared a poem I had written:

FARM WORK: 1960−69

The hotter, the drier, the better.
Hay making time.
Sweat dripping off noses,
An Iowa family puts up the hay.
Baler, driver, loader, unloader, Kool-aid makers.

"She's all done, boys!"
Hickory tree shade.
Pastel, aluminum drinking glasses, sweating like the workers.
A family celebrates.

I was flattered when Sarah read it and, line by line, commented on each idea. "Did you bale the hay?" I responded that we did. She said her father used to put loose hay up in the haymow. I explained that my brother Ed and I were the "Kool-aid makers." Sarah asked about the metal drinking glasses. I described the ones popular in the 1950s: dark blue, purple, deep red, and harvest gold. She said, "They really sweat in the heat. There is *nothing* like cold, icy water when you're putting up hay."

We sat in silence for a moment. Then Sarah said, "Your poem doesn't rhyme but mine does. Yours is prose. It's modern art." She went on to talk about how she writes her poems:

> I write my poems on scraps of paper, wherever and whenever I can. I write about what strikes me; about what I know. I don't do it all in one day. And I find it's a lot like diary keeping. It's best to do a diary entry immediately, now rather than later. With the poetry, it is better to get your thoughts down quickly. If I write on paper in my purse, I can then go back and look at it later. One day I was driving to town with the girls in the buggy. We passed a porch and saw the most unusual, comical sight. On the porch swing sat two guinea hens and a cat, usually not friendly toward one another. I knew I wanted to write about that peaceful scene. So I jotted it on a piece of paper and dropped it in my purse.

Since that day, we have become readers for each other, commenting on what we think our poems say. One cool summer day, we read poetry aloud on the porch swing. We used a brilliant patchwork quilt to protect our backs from the south breeze. We swung to the cadence of a poem I'd written about picking wildflowers as a child.

When I finished reading, Sarah waited a moment and said, "Well, you were in a good mood that day!"

"So, do you have any poems for me to hear?" I asked.

"No, I've been busy canning for winter," she answered, "but just wait until the next time you come!"

PLUCKIT

1 pkg. yeast (1 T.)
1/4 cup warm water
1 cup milk (scalded)
1/3 cup sugar
1/3 cup butter (melted)
1/2 tsp. salt
3 eggs (well beaten)
3 3/4 cups flour (approximately)

SUGAR MIXTURE
3 tsp. cinnamon
3/4 cup sugar
1/2 cup nutmeats

Dissolve yeast in warm water. Add sugar, butter, and salt to make a stiff batter. Cover and let rise. Knead down and let rise again. Roll into small balls of dough. Dip them into melted butter, then roll in sugar mixture. Pile loosely into an angelfood cake pan. Let rise 30 minutes. Bake 40 minutes beginning with 400 degrees for 10 minutes. Reduce heat to 350 degrees and remove the rolls from the pan immediately when done. Serve warm or cooled, and "pluck" or pick up a round roll to eat.

November and December 1976

Monday, November 1, 1976. Many diapers to wash. The laundry dried nicely. I also washed our buggy and the cellar steps, folded & put away wash, & baked pumpkin bars. We all had Schwann's ice cream for supper & fresh bars.

Tuesday, November 2, 1976. Sunny, mild. The wind is a'whistling this A.M. Katie surprised me. I asked her where Mama's nose is, but instead she pointed to her own. First time she did. I baked 7 loaves of bread & ironed. I told Katie to give a kiss. So she took me in her arms and opened her mouth that I could feel her teeth on my cheek! (ha).

Wednesday, November 3, 1976. Eli beheaded the last 10 of our second bunch of fryers, helped pluck them, and after breakfast left for work. I dressed them. We kept 6 for ourselves & took 4 along in evening to ESFs for Wanda. Took ice cream along for Mom's birthday.

Thursday, November 4, 1976. I went to help Susan get ready for church & took Katie along. Mae Faye helped, too. We cleaned basement, upstairs, bath, bed, & living rooms. Katie was a little on the fussy side.

Friday, November 5, 1976. Earl Fishers have sale today. Want to leave for Canada. I stopped @ homeplace to pick up pies to take along to sell at the sale lunch counter and got the news that brother-in-law John Troyer passed away.

Saturday, November 6, 1976. Eli helped me in the house in A.M. We then went to homeplace to help get ready for church. He painted fence posts and I helped prepare eats for Mae Faye to take along for the trip to Missouri tomorrow. Eli & I made gingersnaps in evening.

Sunday, November 7, 1976. All of FBMs family were present at John's funeral. Sad day. We went with Bill Bender. Returned about midnight. Got Katie yet @ ESFs.

Monday, November 8, 1976. I cleaned refrigerator because the milk froze in gallon jug & burst scattering contents. Washed in P.M. Diapers dried well. Eli picked up Wanda's table that we used on north porch.

Tuesday, November 9, 1976. I picked up Eli at work & together we went up to Jacobs for dinner. Guests present were all of EFMs' boys & Katie homeward bound from Missouri. In P.M. we helped at Dan Brennemans, who moved to homeplace today.

Wednesday, November 10, 1976. Up early & early breakfast. Eli left for Missouri with Jonah Fisher & other men to help Lyn. They cut wood & did carpenter work. I ironed, mended, & enlarged dresses of my everyday ones. He returned after I was in bed.

Thursday, November 11, 1976. I potted geranium & Star of Bethlehem slips & also covered some of the cans with contact. In P.M. I altered 3 everyday aprons from belts to tie aprons.

Friday, November 12, 1976. Today my wedding dress was enlarged and my purple suit refixed. Now I can get in & have more room. But it's dirty & needs to be cleansed (the dress). Cleaned living room before supper.

Saturday, November 13, 1976. In A.M. I baked 7 loaves of bread, pies, & rolls & cleaned. Took off to get Eli at work. Went to Lloyds for dinner. Eli helped put up wallboard in dining room. Earls were here in evening, visited & got 2 gallons molasses.

Sunday, November 14, 1976. Sunday School attendance: 121. Lesson: Acts 13. We went to Jacobs for dinner. Heard Richard Beilers have a baby girl, Dorothy.

Monday, November 15, 1976. South wind, nice day. I fed hens & raked leaves after breakfast, made up a batch of vegetable beef soup & peeled apples. Katie & I had a lot of fun after dinner. I'd spin the top & she'd return it to me sometimes saying, "Thank you" in her way.

Tuesday, November 16, 1976. We're out of rain water so I washed with hard water. It took a lot of time to heat it on the stove and Tide to launder. I folded and put away wash.

Wednesday, November 17, 1976. Katie & I went to Kalona. She stayed at my folks while I shopped in A.M. & went to Dr. Ballter. We were at my folks for dinner. In P.M. Mom & I visited.

Thursday, November 18, 1976. I hung out Sunday clothes and ironed. Now I've got some clean suits to crawl into after I'm done wearing black. Sunday cap was made for Katie by Mother.

Friday, November 19, 1976. I bought some garage sale items from Lester Mae. I helped Susan in P.M. by cleaning for church Sunday.

Saturday, November 20, 1976. Eli worked at shop in A.M. After dinner he really worked. He hauled and spread barn & henhouse manure on the garden by wheelbarrow & plowed the patch & garden. I trimmed raspberry plants, raked, & hemmed up Katie's black Sunday dress.

Sunday, November 21, 1976. To gma we go @ homeplace. Elmers served eats in basement of Daddy house [the large, main house] where church was held. Lesson: Hebrews 11.

Monday, November 22, 1976. I felt so tired so sat down & peeled apples. Chocolate cake, pumpkin custard, apple crumb pie, apple jello salad were made today besides cooking potatoes in the jacket & apples with cinnamon candy. Eli had an accident on way to work.

Tuesday, November 23, 1976. Last evening Charles Gs of Indiana stopped in. Eli spent most of the day on the couch. His right ankle is bandaged. Shorty fell on it yesterday. Some ligaments are torn. I washed & chored. For first time, Katie carried items from Daddy to Mama by command.

Wednesday, November 24, 1976. Can't get as much of my work done with chores to do. I ironed & got meals & swept.

Thursday, November 25, 1976. Warm after sundown. We went to Sam Millers for a family get-together before Luke Gingeriches' move to Canada. We had good eats and sang in P.M. Grace gave as a remembrance a glass fruit bowl with stand to Eli.

Friday, November 26, 1976. Eli picked up aprons & I remade 4 everyday ones with strings & broadened them. In evening by lantern light I clipped down rose bushes & flower stems. We had fritters for dinner.

Saturday, November 27, 1976. 14/0 [fourteen degrees above zero]. Northwest wind. What do you know! A white blanket of snow. Eli went to Dr. Ballter's office where his bandage was removed. Isaac T. took him. I did Saturday cleaning & patched in evening.

Sunday, November 28, 1976. 0/5. I chored and made breakfast. Then we went to last day of Sunday School. Cold. Were at Neal & Mae Ellens for dinner. I made ice cream in evening.

Monday, November 29, 1976. 0/7. After milking & feeding stock I washed. Got cold hands by hanging up clothes. Hauled 4 loads of manure by wheelbarrow & baked 7 loaves of bread. Eli went to work again in morning with Isaac T.

Tuesday, November 30, 1976. 3/0. Snow remains. Luke Gingeriches' sale today. I chored, hauled 2 wheelbarrow loads of manure, & 8 bushels of oats from turkey house to barn, sacked scattered pig feed, & folded wash.

Wednesday, December 1, 1976. After milking & carrying milk over to James Bontragers, eating, & washing dishes, I went out & cleaned the barn, hauling 2 wheelbarrow loads of manure & dropped down 4 bales of hay & 1 straw. In P.M. I sewed on Katie's everyday quilt top (Lone Star).

Thursday, December 2, 1976. A new blanket of snow in morning. I got up at about 5 DST (We didn't change back). I wanted to sew, but what happened? Instead I prepared carrots, eggplant, squash,

& apples & planted more geranium slips & hung up a macrame in Katie's room.

Friday, December 3, 1976. 9/0. Eli milked in morning for first time since his accident. I finally got my ironing done, mended clothes, finished piecing quilt top for Katie's bed, sewed a flannel sheet & a comforter case for Barbara, & got a comforter top ready for Katie.

Saturday, December 4, 1976. 14/0. Had visitors here for dinner. They cleaned, quilted the comforter & sewed it up, made firewood, and shelled popcorn, etc. Very nice over noon hour. ESFs were here, too.

Sunday, December 5, 1976. Church at Peter Bontragers. Dale H. had main sermon.

Monday, December 6, 1976. I sewed two baby kimonos and cut 2 more after supper. I tried to make my own pattern for the blue ones I sewed. Really had a time with the first one. It snowed.

Tuesday, December 7, 1976. 0/12. I washed & hung out diapers, bath towels, & everyday shirt. Had a big wash (61 diapers). Eli & I hung up wash in basement after lines were put up. I sewed 2 yellow kimonos.

Wednesday, December 8, 1976. Temperature this P.M. is 22 on west side of house. Thawed today. I ironed & baked bread & a big batch of mincemeat cookies.

Thursday, December 9, 1976. "Mother Goose" hustled & bustled about to get ready for her party. She cooked & cleaned & put a child's quilt in frame. When all was ready the neighbors came, Mary Bertha & children (minus William), Amoses & Samuels. We had a waffle supper quilting bee & popcorn shelling.

Friday, December 10, 1976. Guess what I did today! I sat down to quilt and as I sat I thought in a pleasant mood. A gift from Rachel last evening was a homemade wastepaper basket which I probably appreciated more than if she had given a boughten one.

Saturday, December 11, 1976. In A.M. I visited Lawrence Rebecca's store & bought flannel, etc. Eli went pheasant hunting. The hunters all were here for dinner.

Sunday, December 12, 1976. We read & rested. In evening we went to Mark & Ermas. Had ice cream and waffles.

Monday, December 13, 1976. The Mrs. sat down & quilted and put in the last stitch in evening. We took it along to Dads for Mom to bind it. We left Katie there, going to Fred Ss for Christmas supper. Via home Blackie ditched us. David S. taxied us home.

Tuesday, December 14, 1976. Felt tired after our dump last evening. Eli was cut in the left ear. I got a big bump on brow. Katie seemed to have no injuries. I answered the family letter & cut some clothes.

Wednesday, December 15, 1976. God is still on his throne. He gave us another brand new day. Mrs. Fisher washed, folded diapers, and other things. In evening we went to view the corpse of Eli Swartz.

Thursday, December 16, 1976. Funeral today of Eli Swartz. I left Katie at Lloyds and went to Iowa City to shop with Isaac Ts. In evening I made 1 baby kimono of white flannel.

Friday, December 17, 1976. Isaac T. took Katie & me to Kalona on his way to get the school bus. We walked from the corner to Dads. I had an appointment with Dr. Ballter. Gained no weight (good). Made party mix in evening.

Saturday, December 18, 1976. Eli went to work in A.M. He brought our rig home having left it there the night of our mishap. Blackie is nervous now. I baked apple & pumpkin pies & cleaned.

Sunday, December 19, 1976. To church we go at Peter Bontragers. Friendly people we have in our gma.

Monday, December 20, 1976. I made raisin bars, pineapple cookies, & baked bread. Also I began a Sunday bonnet in double-knit gray for Katie. Cold and windy in evening but that didn't keep Dan and Wanda at home who came in honor of Eli's birthday.

Tuesday, December 21, 1976. Work on the bonnet continued. I sort of had to feel my way through. Starched & ironed denim for the inside bottom. By evening I had a bonnet 2 sizes (probably) too big for Katie.

Wednesday, December 22, 1976. A nice day. The Mrs. washed and finished Katie's Sunday bonnet by putting on the bow & strips in the back. How long will the little one be able to wear it? 2 years?

Thursday, December 23, 1976. Another big job was begun. I cut & began sewing a Sunday coatie for Katie to match her bonnet. The lining is quilted with foam rubber for insulation.

Friday, December 24, 1976. Further work was continued on the coat. I learned by doing. Got it done in evening. Tomorrow she can wear it. I fixed 3 pair of trousers yet & ironed Sunday clothes.

Saturday, December 25, 1976. We had our Christmas dinner at Joes. Earls were there, too. Mom did not feel well nor help anything in the kitchen that I saw. Katie really liked the boughten grapes that Ann Marie brought.

Sunday, December 26, 1976. We attended church at Joseph Millers. Cold on way home. In evening we read.

Monday, December 27, 1976. Mild day. I added kitchen curtains to the wash & over-aprons. The wash didn't freeze but dried nicely for winter so that I could fold & put wash away. I aired out popcorn in P.M.

Tuesday, December 28, 1976. Cranberry salad & 2 butterscotch pies & a chocolate cake were created in the Fisher Lodge. I also ironed & pressed Daddy's Sunday pants. Mom is in Mercy Hospital, we heard.

Wednesday, December 29, 1976. I made bean-potato salad & candied sweet potatoes for tomorrow's dinner. In P.M. I made a pink double-knit dress for Elmer Ropp's baby, cut a pair of everyday pants & began sewing them for hubby.

Thursday, December 30, 1976. Ugh, cold. Eli returned in morning from Jameses having carried over our milk & was very red-faced. Ann Marie, Susan, & Mae Faye helped me butcher 22 old hens. Katie didn't feel well. She's getting another tooth. Eli found one hen surviving yet!

Friday, December 31, 1976. 0/15. Northwest wind but not windy. Very nice outdoors. Sunny. I'm canning chicken. 4 cans broke in canner out of 21! Disappointing! Katie feels much better today. Her lower left molar is through partially.

November and December 1977

Tuesday, November 1, 1977. Cloudy all day. Dad & Bertha were breakfast guests with us. While I washed dishes Bertha braided Katie. Dad got milk @ Lloyds. Bertha, Ann, Mae Faye, Susan, & I butchered 33 old hens here. Dad got 12 @ $0.75 each. Dad helped pluck & also shelled ground cherries.

Wednesday, November 2, 1977. Cloudy all day. Leaves on south maple are fluttering down. I canned 14 qt. chicken & 7 qt. cream chicken. I had earache. My diapers are low. Haven't washed this week. Eli worked on chest of drawers in evening. It gets monotonous to be in the house so 'twas a pleasant change to be upstairs while he worked.

Thursday, November 3, 1977. Cloudy. Sun peeped a little bit in morning. Katie wants to help dry dishes of her own accord. She helped with breakfast dishes. With her patties in mine we fluted a pie shell & beat an egg. I baked 2 cherry & 1 shoofly pies [similar to pecan pies]. Went to ESFs in evening for Edna's birthday.

Friday, November 4, 1977. The prettiest morning of all week! The sun is shining, clear blue sky, & wind from east through kitchen [picture of window]. I can see Lloyd's blades of grass (rye or wheat?) now up. Almost looks like spring.

Saturday, November 5, 1977. Eli went pheasant hunting with Jacob & Dale in A.M. Came home—no bird. Larry Bs was meeting place where Dale was choring while Larrys were gone to Canada. They came home this A.M. having bought a place there.

Sunday, November 6, 1977. Church was at Michael Ys. I got to eat at last table [meal is served in shifts to accommodate numbers]. Had sweet potato pie. Tasted about like pumpkin pie. We went to Fred & Leahs, but they weren't home. Then went to Chesters for supper.

Monday, November 7, 1977. Eli went to work & I took buggy on to FSFs. Baby was fussy before I could get to helping butcher chickens. Susan & M. Faye furnished dinner in big house. Dad, Bertha, Ann Marie there, too. Cloudy.

Tuesday, November 8, 1977. I prepared bread dressing, baked bread, made potato salad, cooked tapioca adding jello, and made sugar cookies. In P.M. I finally began washing and was at it when Eli came home.

Wednesday, November 9, 1977. Windy and cloudy. Today is butchering day here for the 20 old hens & 4 dressing roosters. Only one that showed up was Ann Marie! But we managed. Was about 5:30 when we finished. Melted fat afterwards.

Thursday, November 10, 1977. Ooh cold! I was outdoors hanging up wash when sister Mae of Buchanan arrived for a short day. She washed breakfast dishes for me. I canned 14 qt. chicken. We ate dinner and visited. She left about 2:30.

Friday, November 11, 1977. Went to ESFs to help get ready for church. Barbara was very fussy A.M. Is teething. She slept well in P.M. I made apricot pies and helped prepare tables downstairs.

Saturday, November 12, 1977. Lovely day. Eli plowed garden. I canned cream chicken & washed buggy.

Sunday, November 13, 1977. Chilly. Went to church at Eli's folks. Was well attended. Sermons by Ed T. & Jerome B. Barbara liked sitting on Andy Vera's lap in P.M. Katie and Fannie played together.

Monday, November 14, 1977. Very nice morning. I washed dishes from yesterday and washed. In P.M. Mae Ellen H. took me to Kalona. Girls were at Lloyds. Spent $51.00 at grocery store! Got chicken ground @ Super Valu for bologna.

Tuesday, November 15, 1977. Nice morning. I hung up clothes after breakfast. We females visited Fellowship School in first period. At recess Irma pushed Katie on swing. She enjoyed the ride. Went to Jeremiah's store & later bought celery at Bill Fs.

Wednesday, November 16, 1977. Cloudy, rain in P.M. Children & I were out b-4 the school bus went. I was raking. Canned 7 qt. chicken bologna and ironed. Also cooked apples and potatoes. Baby had only 1 nap today.

Thursday, November 17, 1977. Windy. I raked in morning. Girls looked out bay [picture of window] @ Mama [Sarah herself]. Planted peach stones, dug canna bulbs, patched wash house [picture of door] with board, & greased hoe & spade. Sam Miller is hospitalized. Was in wreck today.

Friday, November 18, 1977. So beautiful in A.M. I made a yellow duck & a man's head from noodle dough before making noodles. Katie said, "Dot Mann," [that man] before I was done. Tickled me. Made oodles of noodles and raked in evening after [picture of sun shining] set with girls out, too.

Saturday, November 19, 1977. About 4:20 I was up. With ourselves & children ready we rode in dark to Brother Jacobs who were still in bed. Sang Happy Birthday outside bedroom [picture of window]. Susan let us in. Had pancakes for breakfast. Eli began work on Dan B's buggy. I cleaned & baked oatmeal cake.

Sunday, November 20, 1977. Church was at Michael Bs. I forgot Barbara's cap! She wore her hood part time or nothing.

Monday, November 21, 1977. Cold, 20. I washed. Had Leanne &

Mary Sue under my charge while James husked corn. Barbara & Mary Sue both got along better than Leanne & Katie. Katie was so grouchy. She slept well in P.M. Leanne got the Etch-A-Sketch. Katie likes it now, too.

Tuesday, November 22, 1977. Baby was fussy in A.M. Is teething. I made 8 loaves of brown bread and remade a blue winter coatie I got @ Erma's store. Katie wore it in evening to Dan Brennemans for Wanda's birthday. Had ice cream.

Wednesday, November 23, 1977. Had a little snow in morning! It was rather late when I got up. Daughters were awake so I put them to bed with Daddy. Hurried to get lunch fixed & was tired after breakfast. Katie got on my back so I gave her a piggyback ride. Barbara has upper left central incisor.

Thursday, November 24, 1977. Thanksgiving Day. Gleaming beautiful day. Wedding of Wilford & Viola. We attended family dinner at FBMs. Had a good dinner and a jolly & noisy time. We visited Sam Miller on the way home. Came home at dark.

Friday, November 25, 1977. Snow on ground in morning. Most we've had so far. Cold and wind from north. I burned trash, dressed the lone lame pullet, fixed the barn door, split wood, set meat jars in place, fed sheep, and ironed, etc.

Saturday, November 26, 1977. Eli went to work. In P.M. he worked on ESFs' crawler @ Gingerich Implement. Came home 5:30. Dan B. came in P.M. to see his buggy. Not much done yet. I canned apple pie filling & ground cherries. Eli worked on buggy in evening. Cloudy.

Sunday, November 27, 1977. Last day of Sunday School. First prize a Bible to Darla Fisher. Wintry outdoors but extra warm in schoolhouse in morning. We were at Jonah Claras for dinner. We had popcorn, oranges, candy & cider in evening. We read.

Monday, November 28, 1977. Don't feel very peppy but should wash. I tried to put in storm windows on north porch alone & got my thumb badly pinched. Managed to get many dishes washed & wash machine put away. Eli brought in clothes.

Tuesday, November 29, 1977. Went shopping at Jeremiah's. Bought a $15.00 gasoline 2-mantle lantern, 3-burner hot plate for $13.50, dark blue scarf, etc. Children stayed @ Isaac Ts. In P.M. I ironed. Eli sawed board for buggy with table saw in turkey house.

Wednesday, November 30, 1977. Nice morning. Snow remains. After getting items organized to take along and children wrapped, etc., it was late, 2:00, until we started for Kalona. Got horse shod & shopped. Went to ESFs for his birthday. Eli came from job.

Thursday, December 1, 1977. So nice in A.M. Sunny & thawing. I sat on bench on south porch & spool knitted! Using the cord I connected a green pair of mittens for Katie, also mended clothes. Cloudy in P.M. Washed Katie & my hair. Barbara is such a heavy chunk.

Friday, December 2, 1977. Nice morning. Snow on ground. Sun shining. 40 in P.M. For first time Barbara got 5 braids instead of 2. 3 on left side and 2 on right. I pieced a red, gold, & white doll quilt, patched trousers & socks on machine.

Saturday, December 3, 1977. Eli didn't have to go to work this morning so we visited about our single days & got up late. Had fried mush, beef (from bones) gravy, & molasses. I made bread and Ranger cookies and cleaned. Eli worked on buggy.

Sunday, December 4, 1977. Church text Matt.: 24−25. Katie & Barbara wore royal blue. Eli brought Katie upstairs asleep & took Baby from me & put her to sleep. How kind! Were @ home in evening and sang hymns.

Monday, December 5, 1977. Another pretty blanket of snow. The gray woods & falling snow make a wintry scene through bay window. Baby says "Da" and baby talk. She stands alone.

Tuesday, December 6, 1977. Drifts, cold, 0/8. Northwest wind. [picture of sun shining and line curving over it] Sun dogs [small halos] arc above sun. We have a dry place to be and fuel for warmth. Much to be thankful for. From a gray pair of dress pants I made a complete dress. They had cost $0.20 at Grace's store.

Wednesday, December 7, 1977. Barbara and Katie wore their dark "pants" dresses I made. I was very pleased with them, although changes will probably be made in the next ones. I washed. Sunny and wind changed to southeast.

Thursday, December 8, 1977. God is giving us more snow this morning. Baby & Katie call back and forth reminding me of chickadees. Baby has bottle & lies on green rug in front of sofa while Katie plays with dominoes at table.

Friday, December 9, 1977. Cold—2 above was highest. Snow drifted all day. At evening wind died down. Baby was given a hard-boiled egg to play with @ supper table. Dear child. I ironed, took care of children and fixed clothes.

Saturday, December 10, 1977. Snow all around and brightly shone the sun. Eli made a hammer & pegs for Katie's peg bench. She enjoyed sitting & pounding. I opened seams on clothing to fix & sewed a dark green dress for Barbara.

Sunday, December 11, 1977. Remember the Sabbath Day to keep it holy. Six days shalt the labor & do thy work. We sang, read, & prayed. Children played. Eli & I pieced puzzles. In evening after girls were in bed I read from *Family Life* to Eli.

Monday, December 12, 1977. Thawing. I washed. Most of it dried that hung outside. In P.M. I baked 7 [picture of bread loaf], broadened Barbara's everyday coatie, & sewed on snaps, folded wash, & washed many dishes. Tragedy: Mark Beiler was killed this P.M.

Tuesday, December 13, 1977. Snow drifts are too dirty & wet for real snow building. Grass shows. I sat outdoors to do writing with Barbara's company in stroller also on south porch. Katie played with a ball & wagon. I ironed.

Wednesday, December 14, 1977. James Rebecca left Mary Sue here & took eats to Fellowship School. I worked up squash and canned 18 pt. In evening Eli & I viewed the body of Mark Beiler in funeral home. Sad.

Thursday, December 15, 1977. I canned 13 pt. squash. Have 31 pts. in all now. Also canned dried kidney and soybeans and spuds. Katie was outdoors with me b-4 dinner. I cleaned north part of barn & burned trash. Thawing snow.

Friday, December 16, 1977. Mild, thawing. The girlies & I went to ESFs. I stopped in and took Emmanuel Leah along. We quilted on Eli's everyday brick-colored quilt with avocado lining. Dan B. came in evening and helped Eli work on buggy.

Saturday, December 17, 1977. Lot of snow gone. Raining & cloudy in morning. For once I did better house cleaning on Saturday and rearranged furniture in living room. Children and I had baths before supper. Eli washed supper dishes.

Sunday, December 18, 1977. David Overholt had church. Peter and David T. preached. After church we went to Fred and Leahs who were at Al Fishers. They had gma, too. Were there for supper.

Monday, December 19, 1977. Mild, damp, snow in evening. At first it looked tapioca-like. Later on was fluffy. I washed and hung most of diapers out. Washed buggy which really needed it. Had supper @ Gingeriches for Gingerich Implement crew.

Tuesday, December 20, 1977. Good washing yesterday. Weather is colder now & snow on ground. I folded wash that had hung overnight in living room & hung up some more. I opened seams on a pair of slacks & cut a dress for Barbara from them. Sewed on it.

Wednesday, December 21, 1977. Husband is gone so much that he can't enjoy sitting in the warmth of the living room on cold wintry days with the family. It gets monotonous without him. And we miss out so much. Sewed dresses for the girlies.

Thursday, December 22, 1977. I decided to take the dark blue double-knit dress made from slacks for Katie because it was long enough. Did handwork on it and the old gold dress for Katie made from zipper [picture of trousers]. Mae Ellen H. and children were here in evening. She gave date-nut bread & a fish mobile she made.

Friday, December 23, 1977. Under a true blue sky, I shoveled snow after dinner. This really helped me after being tensed up from being a Mrs. Sew and Sew so much this week. A sight to behold was our black and white cat resting on top of curled up Brownie! I made bread, oatmeal bars, & cookies.

Saturday, December 24, 1977. Eli was gifted by a wagonload of red elm firewood from his dad in appreciation for fixing his crawler minus labor charges. Dans & ESFs were here for dinner. Wanda made candy, Edna patched, Leah made grapenuts.

Sunday, December 25, 1977. We attended church at Chester Fishers. Had Christmas story text. Was very cold in P.M. We visited Lois in Kalona after we'd eaten pie at Chesters. Barbara was very spunky during last prayer in church but slept well afterwards.

Monday, December 26, 1977. Cold. Snow still remains. Eli hung out wash. Dan & Wanda were at Jeremiah Bontragers last night & here for dinner.

Tuesday, December 27, 1977. I finished husband's chores and hitched up Blackie. In P.M. we went to Big Isaac & Rosemarys. The girls slept on way over. I bought from Rosemary 30 yards of dry goods @ $37.30. Very good denim @ $2.10.

Wednesday, December 28, 1977. Warmer today, 20 in morning, south wind. I ironed & made myself a white cap. Marigold had a big boy calf with help of vet in evening after supper. Baby stood up by herself this evening and took 2 steps.

Thursday, December 29, 1977. Got to bed late & up late. After hurrying I felt tired. Sat & read from *Youth Companion* & repaired books. Baby is asleep & Katie is errand girl. Pretty day. I cut and partly made a pretty blue double-knit dress for Barbara.

Friday, December 30, 1977. Cloudy & snowed a little. I helped Erma get ready for church. My daughters went, too. Andy Rs, Kayleen, & 3 youngest, too, were there. We had very good apple butter for dinner.

Saturday, December 31, 1977. Eli went to work in A.M. He hitch-hiked home. The chilly wind made him cold. I made bread and finished Baby's dress, also cleaned refrigerator. Eli bathed the girls in evening.

Afterword

Martha's gift to Sarah

Until I met Sarah, there was little I couldn't hurry in my life. In an instant, it seemed, I could revise recipes to cut cooking time, attend two volunteer meetings, clean the house, and return phone calls, all in one evening. I thought I would be rewarded with increased discretionary time. But there never was extra time. Sarah taught me how to write a circle letter, garden with a purpose, and bake pies efficiently. But more than tangible skills, she taught me a virtue: patience.

On one occasion, I arrived at Sarah's home on a bake day. Her daughters were turning out four kinds of berry pies in the bake house. I said to Sarah, "Today I brought you a gift." I noticed that she was wearing her apron and ready to do the breakfast dishes, and so I added, "Oh, and put me to work."

Sarah laughed and said, "No one else has said that this morning." Sarah handed me an apron, and I began drying dishes. When we were finished, I brought out a vase I had made for Sarah, my first project from a beginning ceramics class. As we sat at her dining table drinking instant coffee, Sarah opened the wrapping, held up the vase and said, "You made this with your own hands. This is much too precious. You should keep it."

"But I want to give you something—you're always giving me so much," I said. "You can put flowers in it."

"Or I could put cotton in the bottom and then put pencils in it or use it as a spoon holder. Oh, there are many purposes for this." She set the vase between us on the oak dining table.

I asked, "How do you feel about your new house? It's so roomy and convenient." Sarah continued to look at the vase but said nothing.

I tried again. "It must be exciting to be all moved in."

Sarah said, "I'd have more to say about it if it was done. This house has tried my patience."

"But I think you're always patient. What is patience to you?" I asked.

I try to be patient . . . but I must admit I'm glad the pullets are growing fast
and will be laying eggs soon.—Sarah Fisher

"Real patience is letting go, accepting what you have. Some
people are born with patience, some are not," Sarah said.

I said, "I try to be patient, but it's so hard. Take ceramics. Each
step builds on the one before it: placing the clay in the center of
the surface as it spins, opening the clay, pulling the clay, shaping it
into a bowl. If one part of the process is hurried, it ends up a ru-
ined object. I can't hurry it. Believe me, I've tried."

"Then, Martha, maybe what you're doing is impatiently working on patience! The German word is 'comf' and the English is
'fight.' If we're not born with patience we fight for it, for the self-
discipline it takes to be patient. I try to be patient, too, but I must
admit I'm glad the pullets are growing fast and will be laying eggs
soon. Let's go out and look at them and the garden. Would you like
some early sweet corn and cucumbers?"

On our garden tour I said, "A friend of mine bakes sour cherry
pies every summer but hasn't been able to buy any at the Farmers'
Market. Do you have any sour cherries?"

"Of course. How many gallons do you want?" Sarah asked. We agreed on two gallons, and Sarah spooned them into a container. My mouth watered. I said, "Are you sure you can spare two gallons?" I knew that Sarah baked and sold cherry pies on a regular basis when the fruit was in season.

Sarah put down the large spoon, leaned over, and hugged me. "Of course I can spare two gallons. And I don't know *anyone* who has ever been so happy over sour cherries!"

To recognize and appreciate Sarah's humor, creativity, and compassion through her diary and our conversations has taken me more than an hour, more than an afternoon. It took several seasons. I couldn't hurry our friendship. It took time. Sarah the teacher, quilter, gardener, entrepreneur, and writer demonstrates such an object lesson every time we talk. From Sarah, a woman in a closed society, I have come to understand what a community is and can be. At an evening singing, she and I sat on a bench and shared a hymnal. She whispered to me to start a song. I felt one with the women in their pastel dresses and starched white-net head coverings.

Sarah's actions are windows on her values; her community is the instrument through which she acts on her beliefs. When Sarah says, "I am Amish," she speaks with a sureness of who she is and what is expected of her. My statement, "I am Catholic," does not conjure up the same confidence. Who am I within my community? And what is my community? My church? Workplace? Neighborhood? How do these disparate portions of my life come together? I worry. But maybe I worry a little less for knowing Sarah.

Perhaps it is Sarah who has nudged me into exploring the spiritual dimensions of my life as a Catholic. I said yes when asked to be a teacher for the sacraments of Reconciliation and First Eucharist. Sarah often says, "What could be more important than teaching our children?" I now attempt to visit with friends more often than I used to, though perhaps not with the freedom that

Sarah's strawberry patch.

Sarah does in her community, where dropping in on friends is expected and planning visits is not. I now deliberately seek and collect the stories of these experiences. I treasure and revisit them like a hiker gaining sustenance from a cache of provisions stored on the trail. My stories mirror a tale of searching and constructing an ever-evolving community in my life and learning what it takes to be a contributing member.

And what about Sarah? Does she ever worry about the future? What are her hopes and dreams? I said, "Everything works like clockwork around here. Don't you ever worry about anything?"

"I'm a woman, aren't I? I take a protective approach. I think that women are more this way than men. It's also that I'm more this way as I get older. I've been in a lot of buggy accidents, and I'm scared more than I used to be." English or Old Order Amish, we are all reminded of the fragility of life. Yet, in the risks of daily living, Sarah confidently lives her faith, placing priority on her family and community.

I do not think I'll ever stop learning from Sarah. One evening we sat on a bench facing her west windows, watched the sun go down, and visited while the girls put the finishing touches on supper. Sarah said, "God paints a new sunset each day. Just look at this one. How do the sunsets look in Des Moines?"

I took a deep breath and turned to look at her. "I'll admit I hardly notice sunsets, or sunrises either, for that matter. But I bet I will after tonight," I said.

Now, between our visits, we write letters. In the winter we share opinions on the irresistible promises of the newest seed catalogues. In the summer we visit under the maple tree to share poetry we've written and to take a rest from gardening. Recently I was surprised to see a Frisbee in her yard, which prompted me to tell her of my son Stephen's Frisbee game with friends every Sunday. Sarah immediately invited my husband and son to meet her family. "My children throw the Frisbee well but I can't. So they can play and you and I can cook the food!"

Another day Sarah noticed I was writing in brown ink, one of several colors available from my college bookstore. I asked her if she would like some pens, perhaps to color-code her record keeping. She said, "Maybe." I sent her a packet of seven colors and immediately received a thank-you letter. Each paragraph was written in a different color:

Dear Martha,

Christmas greetings to you.

Well, the busy summer months are behind, the traveling sprees are over, and now I have taken time to pattern our garden and write the recipe for blackberry pie. (Neither of them is perfect.)

We had a pig roast here and then set out for a wedding in Pa. The Lord provided us with a safe trip. We were home to be with family on Thanksgiving Day. So now we're in the last month of the year. What will the next year hold?

It's been quite awhile since I saw you last. Recognize my pens?
(picture of a smiling face)

God bless you and your family.

Bye,
Sarah

P.S. Martha, you've stepped inside my shoes. Stop by anytime to visit.

Works Cited

Bender, David. "Me, Myself, and I." *Family Life* (July 1995): 6–8.

Fishman, Andrea. *Amish Literacy: What and How It Means.* Portsmouth, N.H.: Heinemann, 1988.

Frey, J. William. *A Simple Grammar of Pennsylvania Dutch.* Lancaster, Pa.: Brookshire Publications, 1985.

Hostetler, John A. *Amish Society.* 4th ed. Baltimore: Johns Hopkins University Press, 1993.

Kachel, Douglas. "The Memoriam Poetry of the Old Order Amish." Grandview College, Des Moines, Iowa, 1996. Photocopy.

Safford, Carleton L., and Robert Bishop. *America's Quilts and Coverlets.* New York: E. P. Dutton, 1980.

Selected Bur Oak Books of Related Interest

Tales of an Old Horsetrader:
The First Hundred Years
By Leroy Judson Daniels

"This State of Wonders": The
Letters of an Iowa Frontier
Family, 1858–1861
Edited by John Kent Folmar

Up a Country Lane Cookbook
By Evelyn Birkby

Was This Heaven?
A Self-Portrait of Iowa
on Early Postcards
By Lyell D. Henry, Jr.

Weathering Winter:
A Gardener's Daybook
By Carl H. Klaus

The Wedding Dress: Stories
from the Dakota Plains
By Carrie Young